THEMATIC CHESS TRAINING 11

ANTONIO GUDE

THE PROBLEMATIC PIECE

128 THEMATIC EXERCISES FOR STRUCTURED TRAINING

EDITORA

SOLIS

2023

© Antonio Gude 2004
© 2023 of the English edition by Garcez Leme & Associados, Lda.
Editors: Francisco Garcez Leme and Jussara Chaves Garcez Leme
Layout: Heloísa Chaves Garcez Leme
Published in Aveiro, Portugal in 2023
ISBN: 9786598628154

SUMMARY   **PAGE**

INTRODUCTION

Theory establishes didactic models in the treatment of positions, or in the study of different technical themes, but practice is responsible for creating chaos with its diversity, which is precisely one of the great attractions of chess.

The *Chess School* manuals (1 and 2) have a strong practical orientation, as shown by the fact that, in addition to the numerous positions commented on in the main body, both books contain an additional block of 160 and 128 exercises, respectively.

Nevertheless, the effort to systematize the material, reducing it to valid models, for the sake of the best possible didactic orientation, is not enough for the player to grasp the variety and richness of competitive chess.
This editorial initiative responds to the active player's need to cultivate systematic training, and these books, with 128 exercises each, at three levels of difficulty, will contribute to solving this aspect, because they are theme parks, with positions that expand on monographic aspects developed theoretically in the manuals.

Each book is divided into sections, and the exercises in these sections are rated with one, two or three stars, according to the degree of difficulty, in line with the technique used in *Chess School* (1 and 2).
Measuring the difficulty of an exercise is not easy. Not just because the objective assessment is difficult in itself, but because the degree of difficulty is different for each person. The aim of these books is to reach as many chess players as possible, because that is the only way to justify their publication. In general terms, I believe that the resolution time should be:

First level	★	(1 star)	1- 3 minutes
Second level	★★	(2 stars)	5 -10 minutes
Third level	★★★	(3 stars)	10 -20 minutes

There's no need to be too strict about the reflection time. Self-taught players can be guided by this estimate, while - as we suggested in *Chess School* - the ideal is for the coach to set the exact amount of time for each exercise or block of exercises for a group of players or a specific player.

THE PROBLEM PIECE

The theme of the problem piece, only dealt with in the manuals, is of fundamental importance because of its strategic and tactical repercussions on the game. "One misplaced piece and the whole position is bad," said Tarrasch in one of his definitive and radical statements.Without going to that extreme, in today's chess, where players are used to detecting the slightest favorable or unfavorable nuances, the existence of a problem piece can compromise or limit a player's entire position and the exploitation of this fact by the opponent can be the path to victory.Chapter 5 of Chess School 2 contains a detailed study of the different cases of a problem piece. In this booklet we will group the exercises into four chapters, with very interesting cases of pieces whose situation on the board is negative.

Only one formula is known for progressing in chess: play as many games as possible, together with theoretical study and analysis of the games themselves. The ideal complement to this formula is, as many great masters recommend, for the player to develop and perfect their tactical and strategic skills by solving numerous exercises, specially selected for their usefulness. Like the ones we offer here

1 - The helpless piece

1 - White plays ★

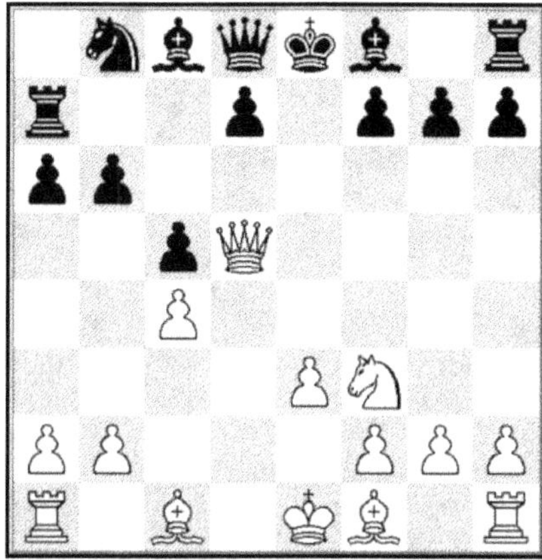

Attacking on the a8 Rook, Black replied ...♖a7. Was that a good idea?

3 - Black plays ★

White has just played **52...♔c6**. Is there any way to tip the scales?

2 - Black plays ★

The Black have a theoretical advantage, but they've forgotten an elementary detail.

4 - White plays ★

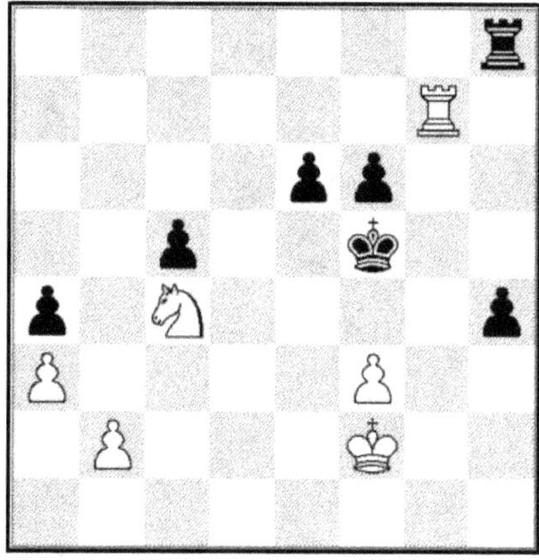

In material terms, the Black have hopes. In positional terms, no. Why not?

1 - The helpless piece

5 - White plays ★★

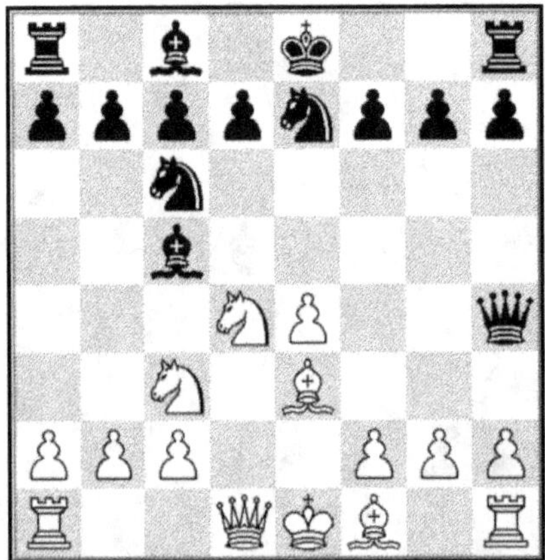

In this position of the Scottish Opening, Black has just played **6...♔ge7**. Why is this a blunder?

7 - Black plays ★★

With a simple calculation, Black wins material in this position and you will have to demonstrate how.

6 - Black plays ★★

The Black have an unexpected continuation here, and it's gaining ground. Which one?

8 - White plays ★★

What is the strongest move in this variant of the King's Gambit?

1 - The helpless piece

9 - White plays 

White has a material and positional advantage, while Black has a displaced Rook. How to take advantage?

11 - White plays 

Can we have a piece? What is certain is that a small detail needs to be resolved.

10 - White plays 

Notice the harmony of the White position and the mismatch of the Black pieces. Act accordingly.

12 - White plays 

The Black position looks solid, but in its field lies a defenseless piece. Take advantage of this!

1 - The helpless piece

13 - Black plays ★★★

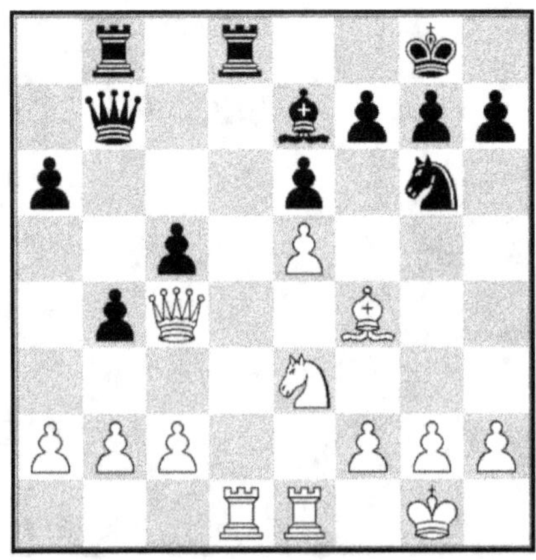

There's a weak link in the chain of White pieces. Try to find a way to break it.

14 - White plays ★★★

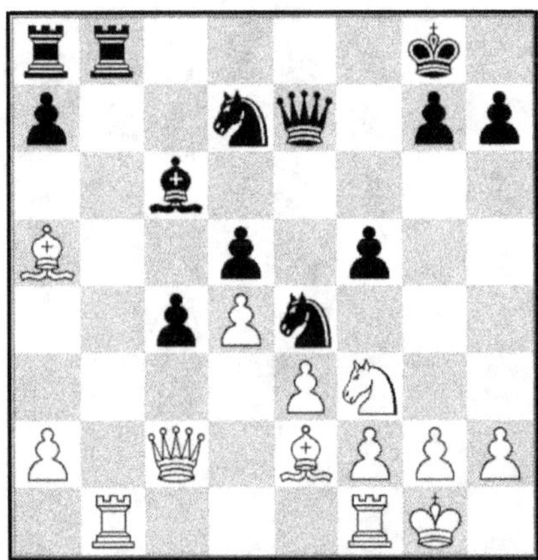

A defenseless piece usually limits the entire position. Your task is to identify it and apply your ingenuity.

15 - White plays ★★★

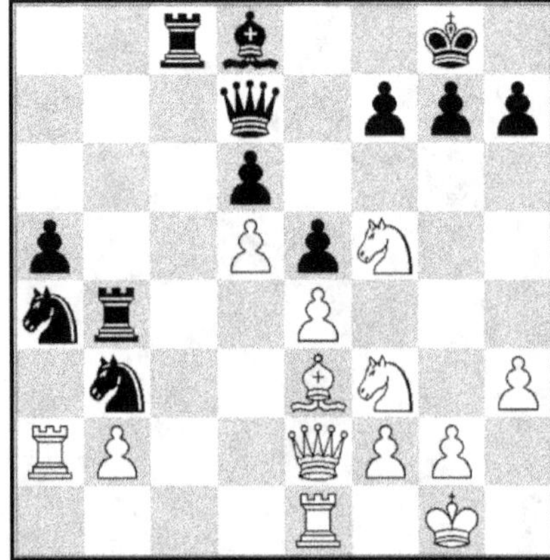

Black dominates in the Queen's wing. But you have larger caliber bullets in the barrel.

16 - White plays ★★★

Veteran GM Miso Cebalo delivers a devastating blow here. I'll say no more.

2. The hunted or closed piece

17 - White plays ★

An easy exercise to practice the ♔+♙ versus ♘ struggle.

18 - White plays ★

A simple combination allows the White to win here cleanly.

19 - Black plays ★

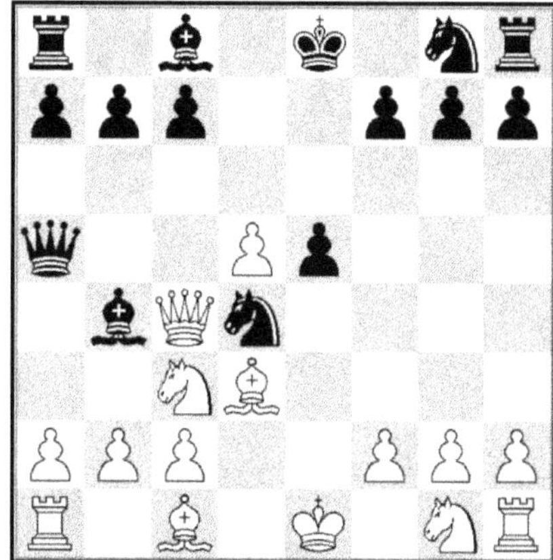

Here you have the chance to get a bigger hunting piece. The little star says it all.

20 - Black plays ★

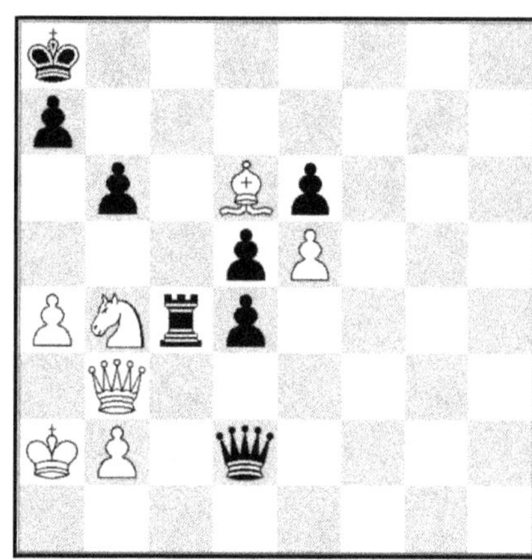

White has just played **44.♘d3–b4**. Why is this a blunder?

2. The hunted or closed piece

21 - Black plays ★

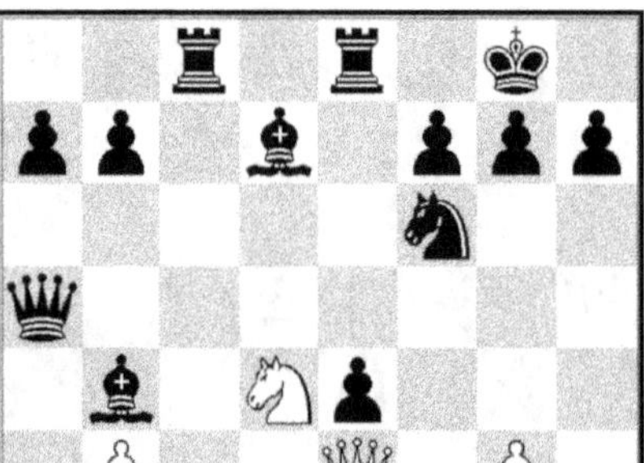

White has just played **17.♛d3–e3**. Do you feel able to exploit your unstable position?

23 - Black plays ★

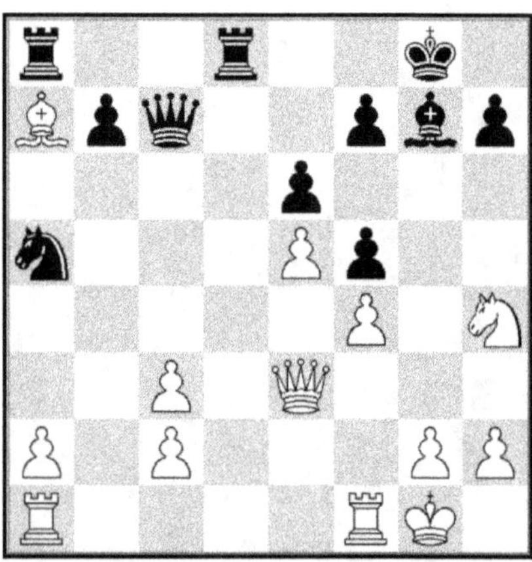

White has just captured the a7 pawn. Does that sound like a good move?

22 - White plays ★

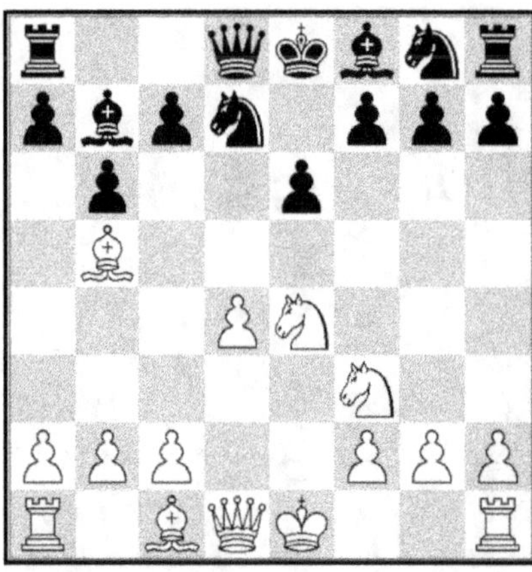

Black didn't play the opening well and his opponent is in a position to refute it. Tell us how.

24 - Black plays ★

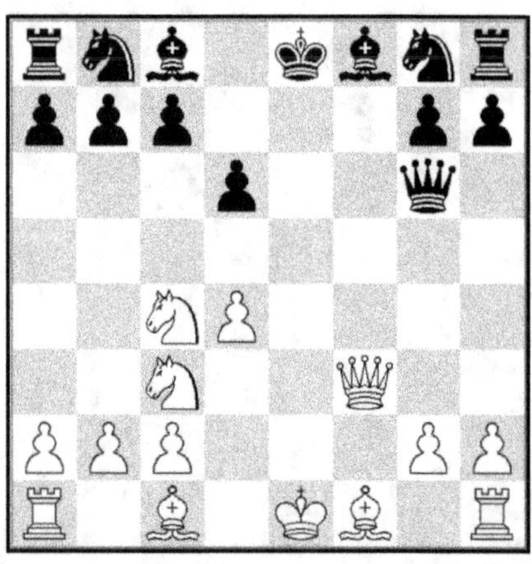

This is a Latvian Gambit position. Can Black take the pawn on c2?

2. The hunted or closed piece

25 White plays ★★

How would you take advantage of White's positional dominance?

27 - White plays ★★

The precise calculation of forced sequences is an essential quality of a good player. But why am I telling you this?

26 - White plays ★★

The great Pillsbury played **19.b4** here. Couldn't he have captured the e6-pawn?

28 - White plays ★★

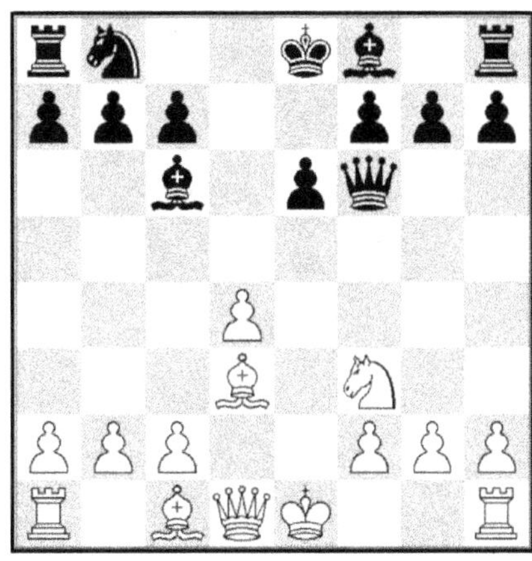

Exchanging Knights on f6, Black took back queenside. But they're in for a major surprise. What surprise?

2. The hunted or closed piece

29 - White plays ★★

Hold on to your hands! The Knight cannot be taken, so find another way to take advantage of your position.

31 - White plays ★★

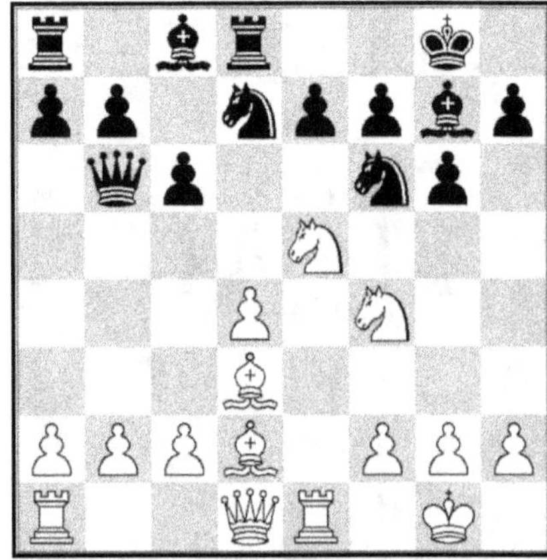

White is developing better, as the Black pieces on the queenside are still in their starting positions. Proposal?

30 - Black plays ★★

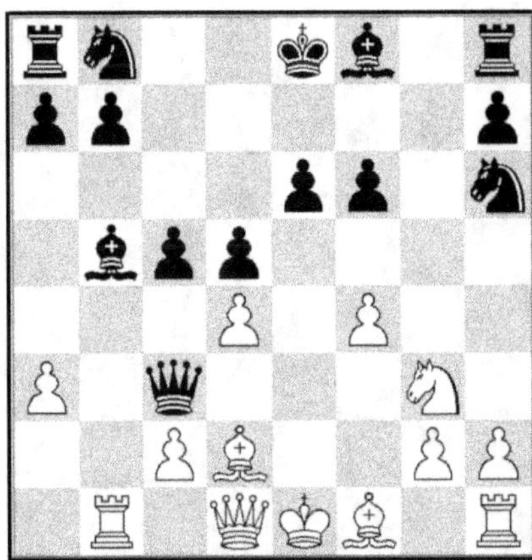

The Black Queen has only two options: capture on d4 or capture on a3. Which one would you be happy with?

32 - Black plays ★★

Will you believe me if I tell you that, as well as being a great strategist, former world champion Tigran Petrosian was a great tactician?

2. The hunted or closed piece

33- White plays   ★★★

The Black Rook carried out an unsuccessful raid. Do you think White can get something by attacking it?

35 - White plays   ★★★

It's not a very easy exercise, but I take your ingenuity for granted. How to win?

34 - White plays   ★★★

A historic encounter. Without any development, the Black and Whites embarked on a dubious adventure. What would you play?

36 - Black plays   ★★★

White has just played **25.♖d7–e7**. What do you think: a hit or a blunder?

2. The hunted or closed piece

37 - White plays   ★★★

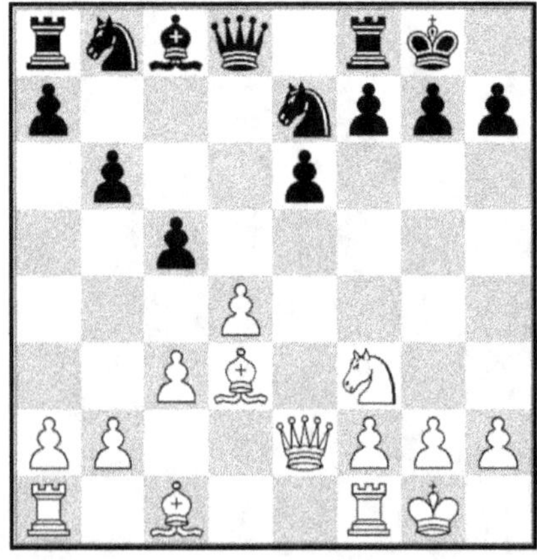

The move ♛c4, with a double attack on h7 and a8, is sung. But the question is: won't the Queen be closed?'

39 - White plays   ★★★

This Rook versus Knight ending is atypical because the Knight is disconnected from the defense.

38 - White plays   ★★★

How would you respond to Black's sacrifice on c3? The intention is clear: if b×c3, ...♛×c3+ and ♛×a1.

40 - Black plays   ★★★

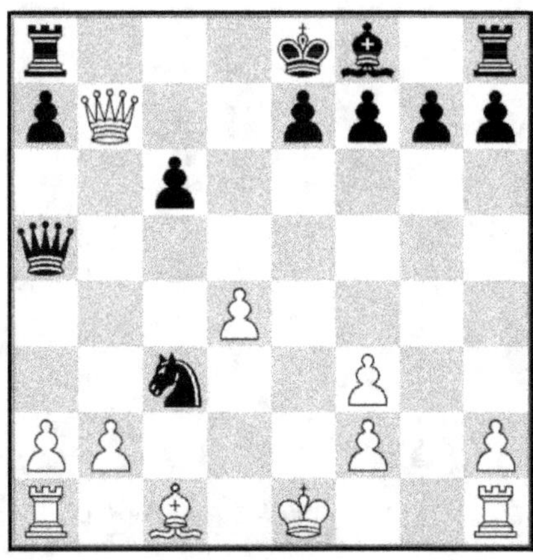

The idea was to capture on c6 and then the Knight, without worrying about the overdraft, which would be followed by ♗d2, but...

2. The hunted or closed piece

41 - White plays ★★★

Two pieces against one and blocked pawns. Can White survive? It's a draw.

43 - White plays ★★★

The Black Queen wants to help defend her castling, but can she help herself?

42 - White plays ★★★

The King in the center shouldn't distract you. There are some dramatic elements here related to overload.

44 - Black plays ★★★

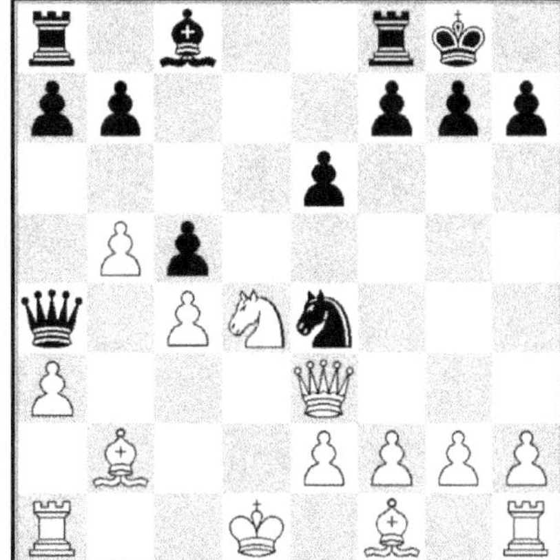

What is the best answer to this question? Naturally, you have to calculate the variants precisely.

2. The hunted or closed piece

45 - White plays ★★★

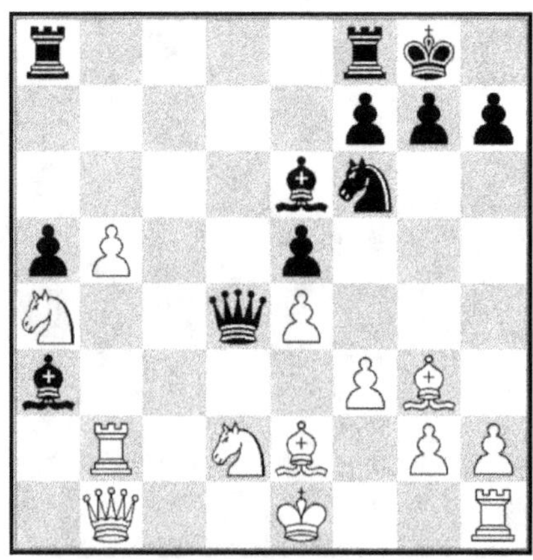

Black's last move, **22.♗a3?**, was very unfortunate, because it decisively compromised his position.

47 - White plays ★★★

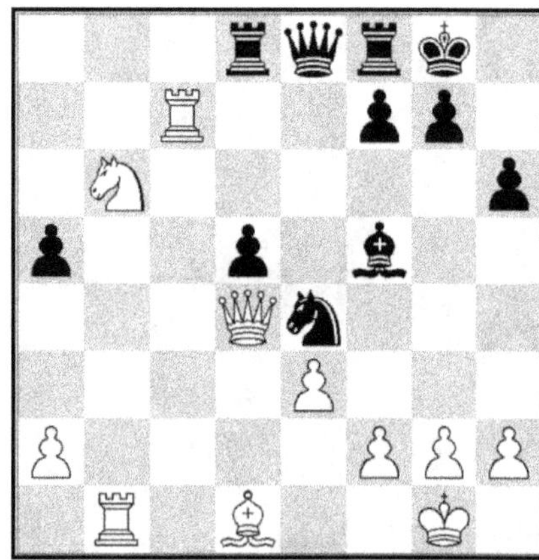

24...♗c8–f5 it wasn't the best possible move. How would you refute it?

46 - White plays ★★★

The black Rook had to block the deadly diagonal **b1–h7**, but isn't it exposed? Of course it has the entire fifth row.

48 - Black plays ★★★

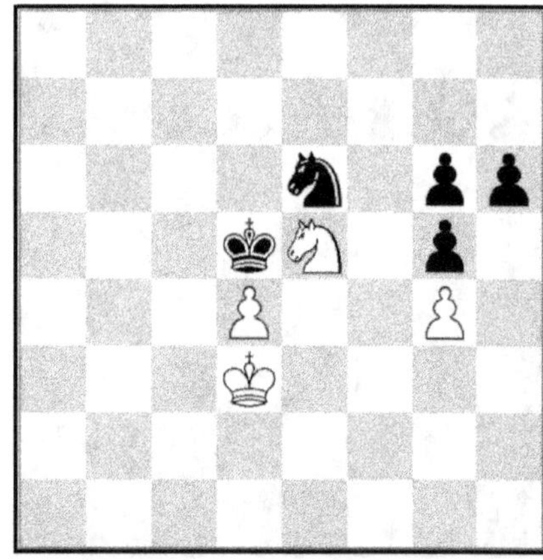

Two monsters of the board argue that this ending looks like a draw. But it only looks that way.

3. The restricted or offside piece

49 - White plays ★★

Faced with the **g5** attack, Black withdrew his Knight to **g8**. How do you win?

51 - White plays ★★

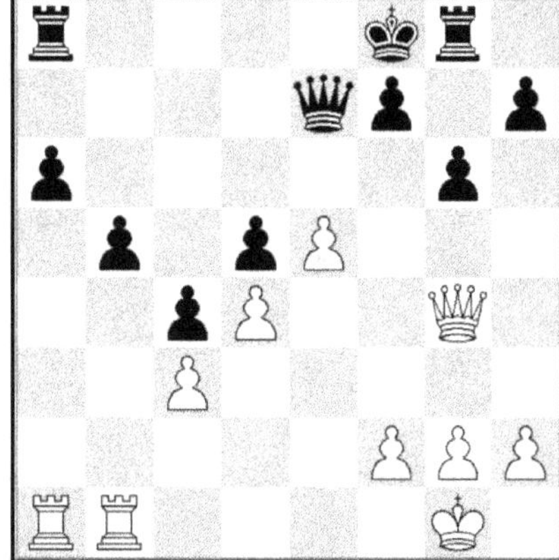

A great artist will explore the momentary passivity of the g8 Rook here. What can you imagine?

50 - White plays ★★

A dubious opening concept allows White to speculate on the paralysis of the restricted piece. How?

52 - Black plays ★★

The White set ♕+♗ is, in this case, a negative battery and the Black set will benefit from this factor.

3. The restricted or offside piece

53 - Black plays ★★

Zugzwang intervenes here to make the White piece useless. But the demonstration is up to you.

55 - White plays ★★

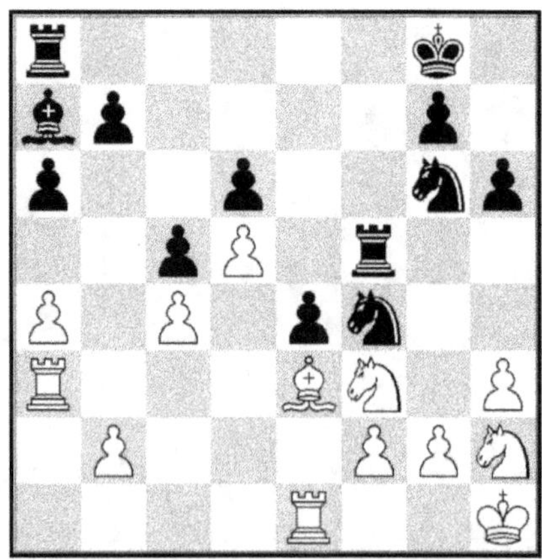

If the Bishop on a7 were on e7 or f6, Black's position would be quite enviable, but the situation is very different.

54 - White plays ★★

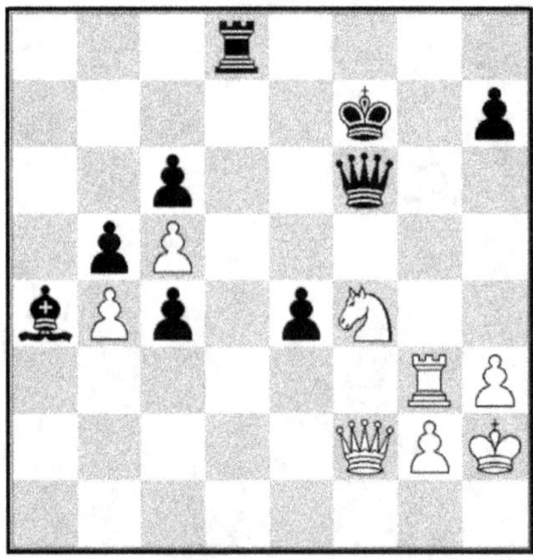

Black's Bishop is in limbo, allowing White to play at will with a piece advantage.

56 - White plays ★★

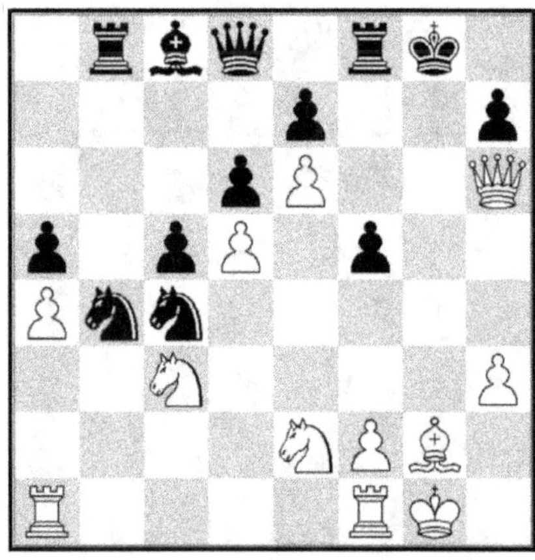

The wedge of White pawns d5+e6 splits the board in two, which, added to the painful bishop on c8, allows for immediate definition.

3. The restricted or offside piece

57 - White plays ★★

The restriction of the Bishop on **b7** together with the weak pawn on **b6** limits Black's entire position. Explore this.

59 - White plays ★★★

The Knight on **h5** is out of the game. This will allow White to carry out a large-scale beneficial operation.

58 - White plays ★★★

How can the White exploit the forced idleness of the opposing Bishop?

60 - Black plays ★★★

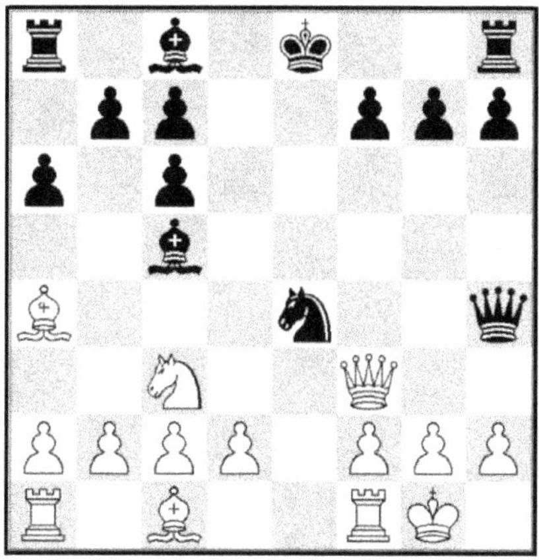

The classic masters knew how to play hard. Here, the Black set off an explosive combination.

3. The restricted or offside piece

61 - Black plays ★★★

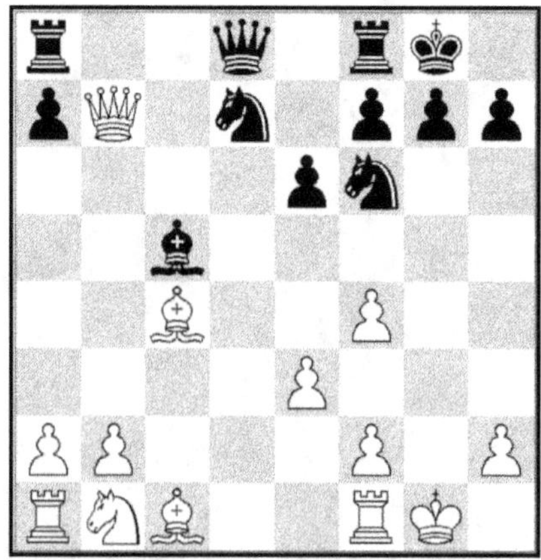

The fragility of the White castling, coupled with his Queen's excursion, suggest diabolical ideas to the Blacks.

63 - Black plays ★★★

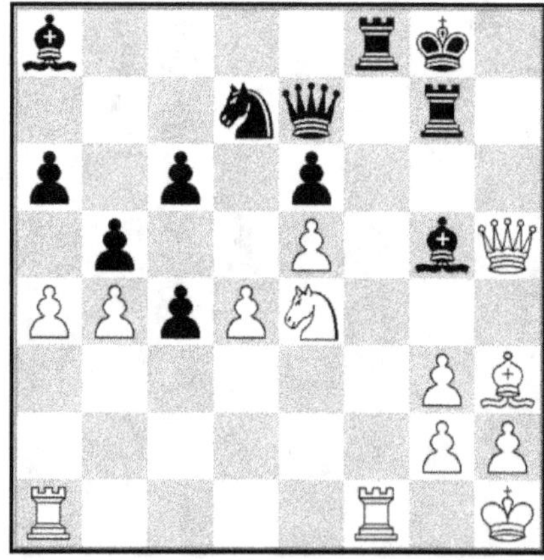

Sometimes there are exceptional circumstances that allow the worst-placed piece to be activated. As in this case.

62 - White plays ★★★

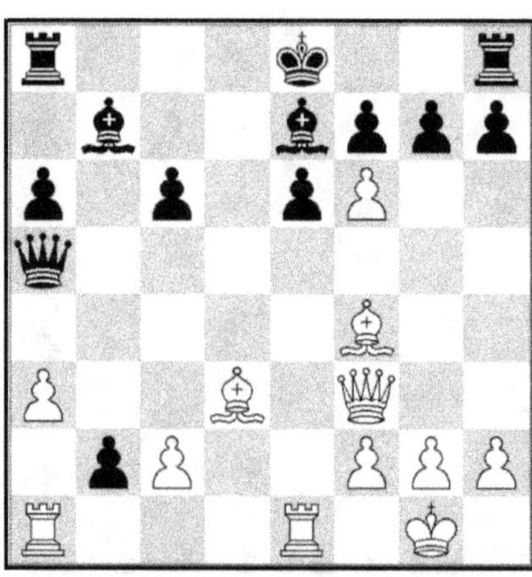

The Black King is in the center and that's important. But it's also important that the Bishop on **b7** doesn't take part in the fight.

64 - White plays ★★★

There is one piece that is absolutely out of play and you won't even be able to smell the gunpowder of combat. Act.

3. The restricted or offside piece

65 - White plays  ★★★

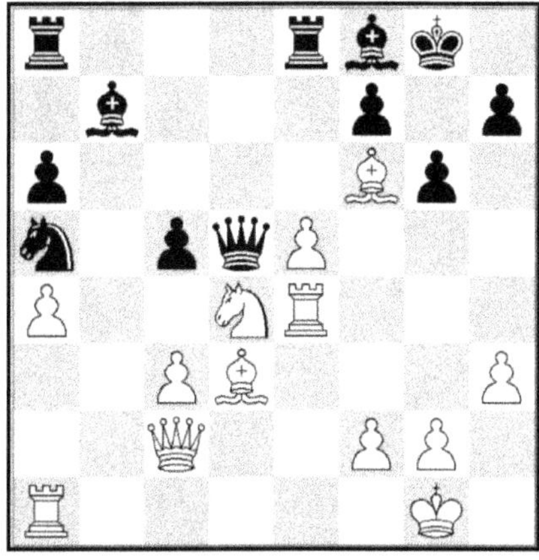

There are several technical problems here, but the most pressing one for Black is that his Knight can't settle. Explore this.

67 - White plays  ★★★

The best way to take advantage of the passivity of the **b7** Black Knight is to play with energy. How?

66 - White plays  ★★★

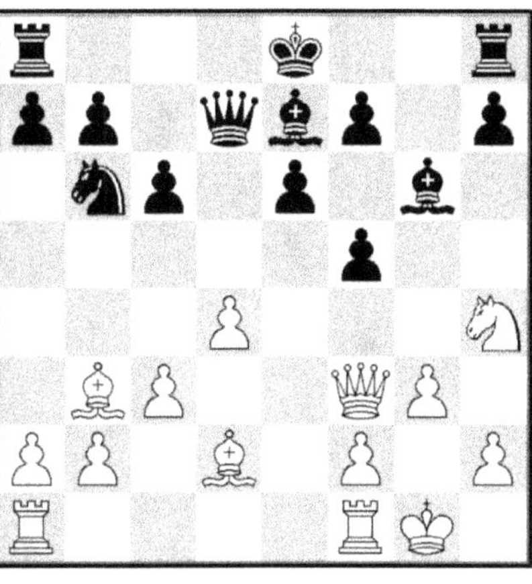

With his last move, **15...f5**, Black ostracized his Bishop on **g6**, which will be felt in the game.

68 - White plays  ★★★

There are other factors, I agree, like the f-file and the passed pawn on e5. But the Black Queen Bishop is a serious weight.

3. The restricted or offside piece

69 - White plays  ★★★

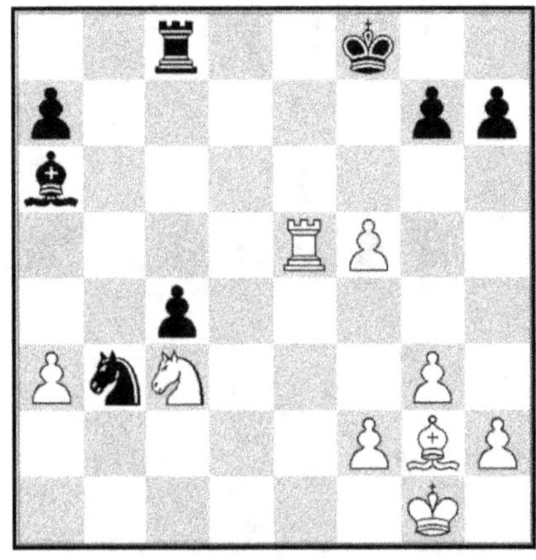

The Black minor pieces are misplaced and, with dynamic play, GM Beliavsky will demonstrate how to win.

71 - Black plays  ★★★

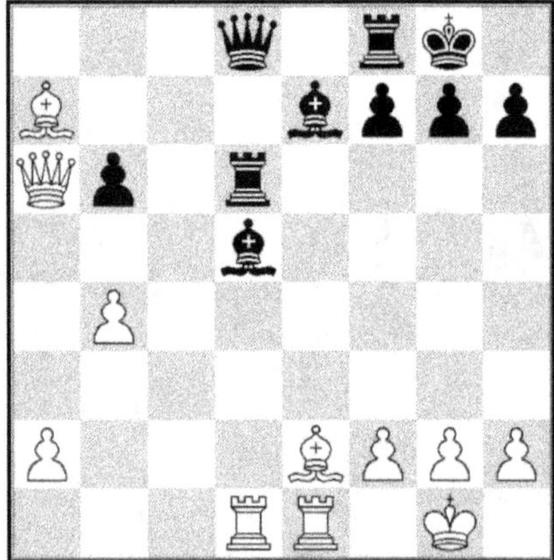

The White player (one of the best in the world) was too optimistic by capturing a pawn on a7. What will happen now?

70 - White plays  ★★★

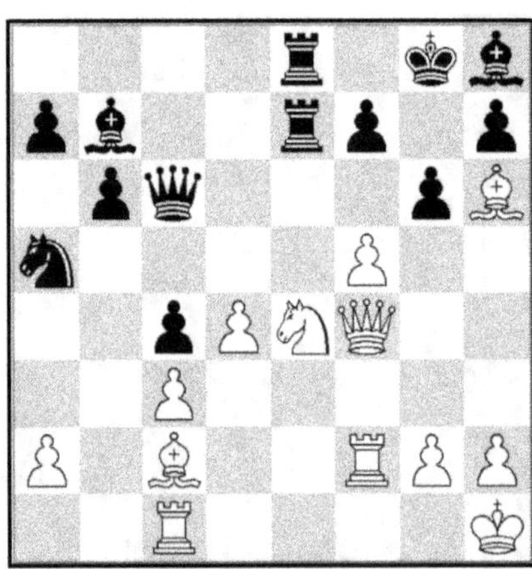

One of those great games of the 20th century. Nothing happens with the Knight on a5. Why is that?

72 - White plays  ★★★

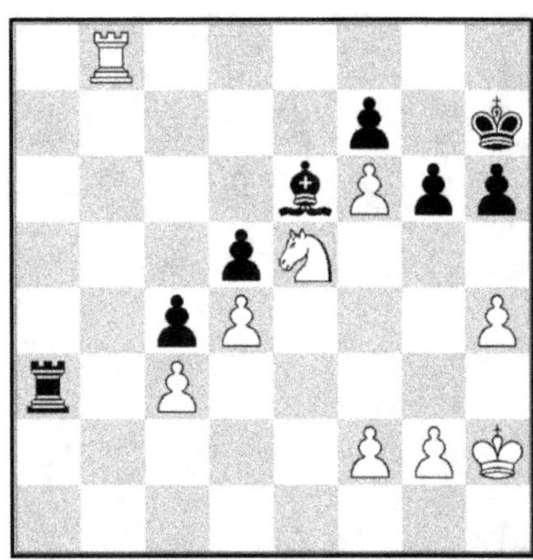

The Black Bishop's torpid situation is the key to the ultimate plan. Can you see him?

3. The restricted or offside piece

73 - White plays ★★★

The two Black Bishops are pitiful and this allows the White to make a clear and effective plan.

75 - White plays ★★★

It's true that White has two magnificent strengths in **d5** and **e4**, but what about the sad Knight on **a5**?

74 - White plays ★★★

The Black pieces are not well coordinated, but the most serious is the situation with the Bishop on **c8**. How would you proceed?

76 - White plays ★★★

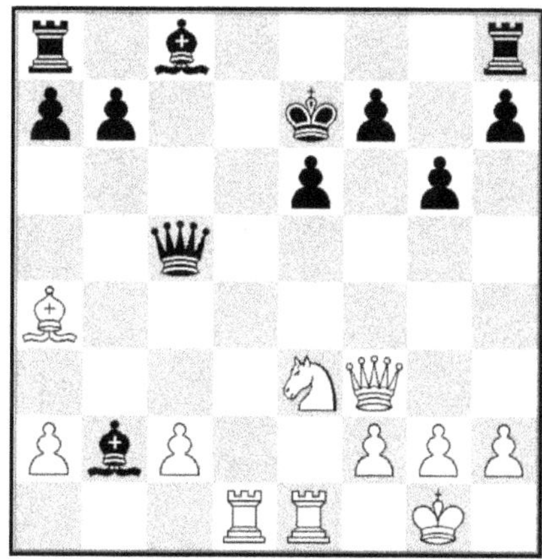

The Black Bishop has captured a pawn on **b2**. How can this capture be punished?

3. The restricted or offside piece

77 - White plays ★★★

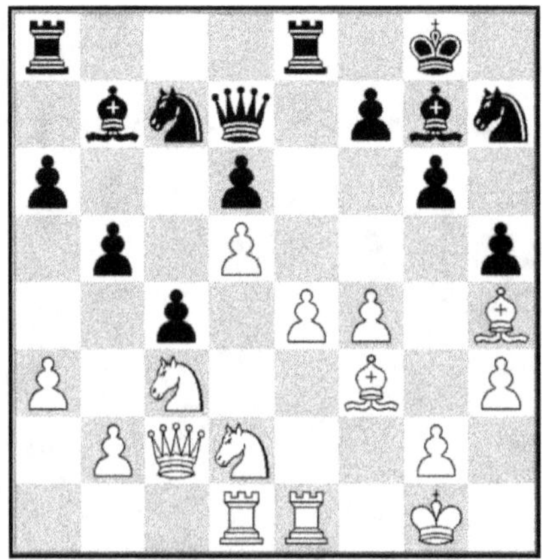

At the start of the half game, another masterclass from Petrosian on how to exploit the opponent's restriction of pieces.

79 - White plays ★★★

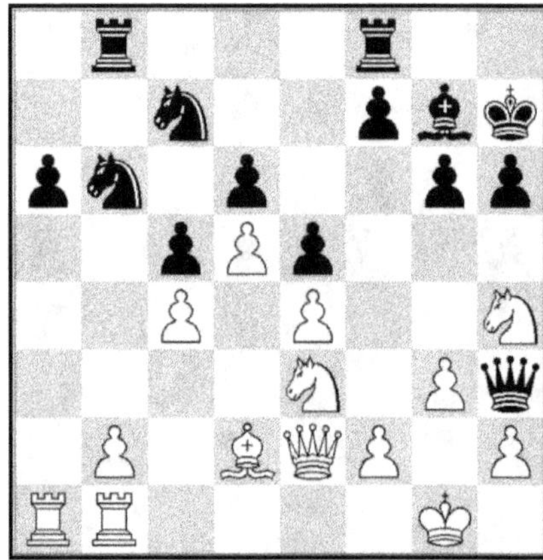

It's not easy to see how to exploit the restricted pieces here, but a ward action will shed a lot of light on the matter.

78 - Black plays ★★★

With one piece missing, two pieces out of play. Too much of an advantage for a world champion.

80 - White plays ★★★

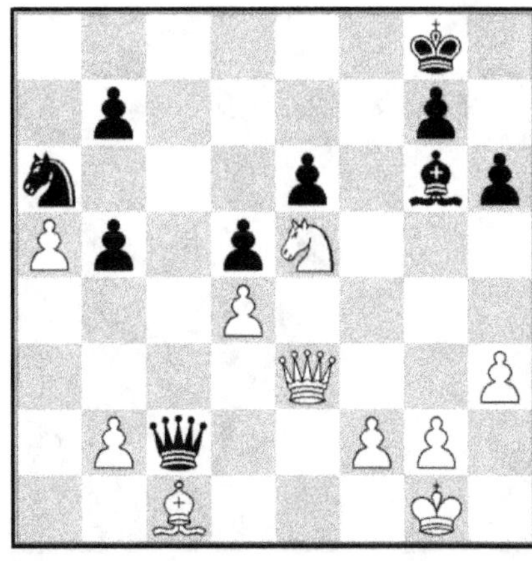

The proposal is very simple: it's about preventing the Black Knight from playing again in the whole game.

4 - The overloaded piece

81 - Black plays   

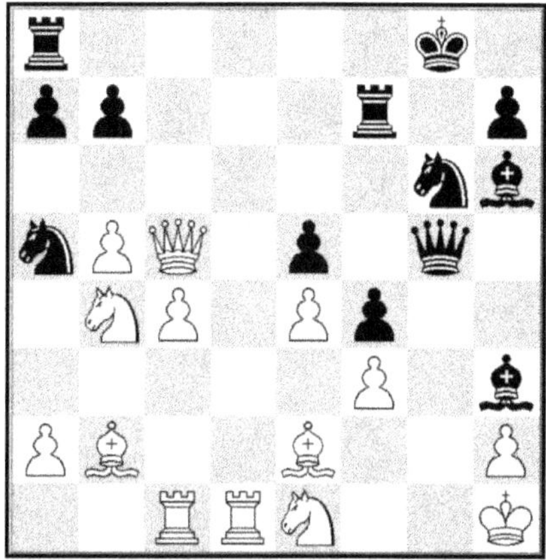

The arrangement of the White pieces allows your opponent to win material easily. How?

83 - Black plays ★

Even if it doesn't seem like it at first glance, there is a seriously compromised part. How do you win?

82 - White plays ★

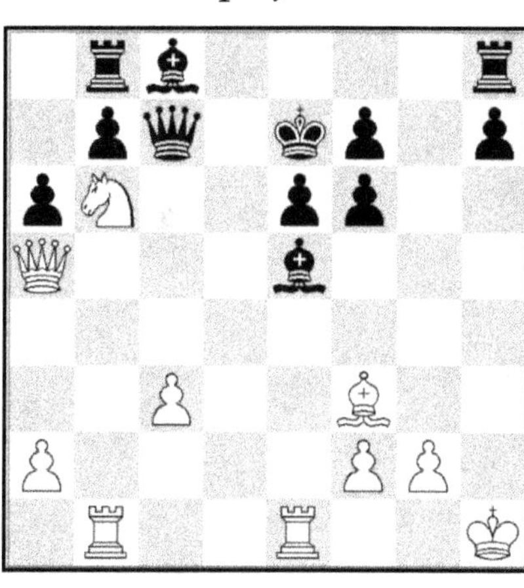

Even if it's easy, the loser is a world champion (but the game is a rapid).

84 - White plays ★

There's only one way to win, and you have to play it with mathematical precision.

4 - The overloaded piece

85 - White plays ★★

The last move was **27...♗c5?**. How can White tip the scales in his favor?

86 - White plays ★★

In this variant of the Scandinavian Defense, **6...♛b6×b2?** is a serious mistake. Why and what is the correct move?

87 - White plays ★★

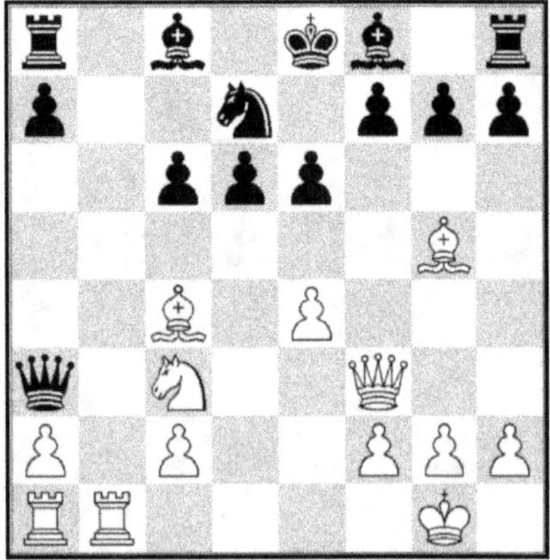

The Black Queen is in an unstable position. How can we take advantage of it?

88 - White plays ★★

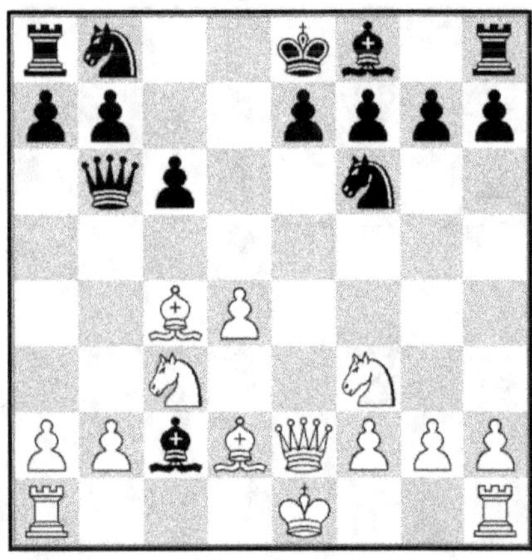

The capture **9...♗×c2** is exploitable according to opening theory. How should White play?

4 - The overloaded piece

89 - White plays ★★

You can't win with ♖h8+ or e6, but there is a way to exploit the situation of a Black piece.

91 - Black plays ★★

When the Knight attacked, Black drew his Queen on d2 (9.♕d1 was better). Why is this a big mistake?

90 - Black plays ★★

The White seem to have a more than acceptable position, but that of one of their pieces is questionable. What do you think?

92 - Black plays ★★

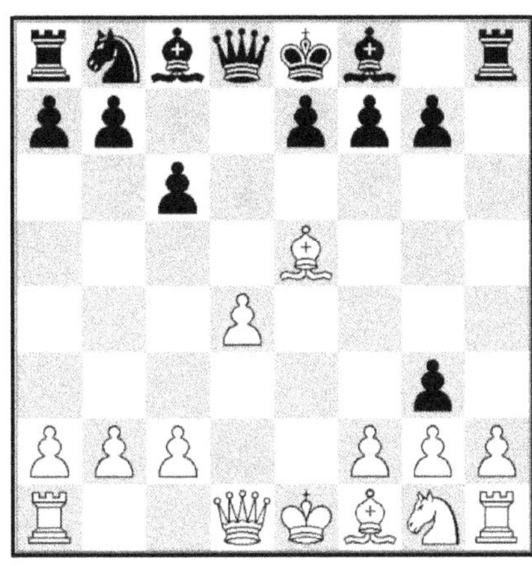

Theoretical trap by Caro-Kann. Black played **8.♗f6−e5**. How should the game go?

4 - The overloaded piece

93 - White plays ★★

Will you be able to figure out how to save this thorny ending? If so, congratulations!

95 - White plays ★★

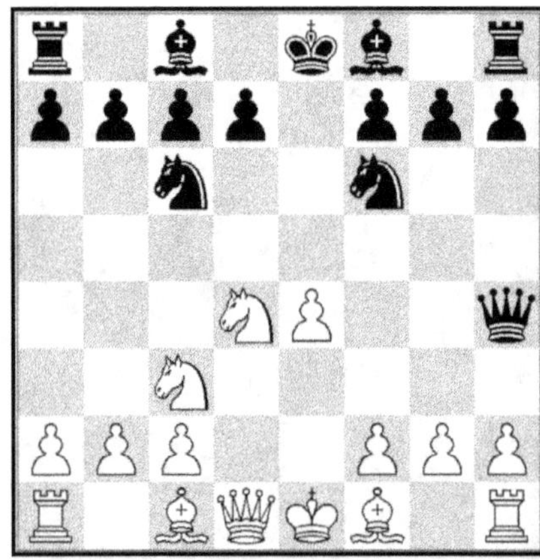

Position of the Steinitz Variant in Scottish, after **5...♘f6?**. How to refute this move and what was the correct alternative?

94 - White plays ★★

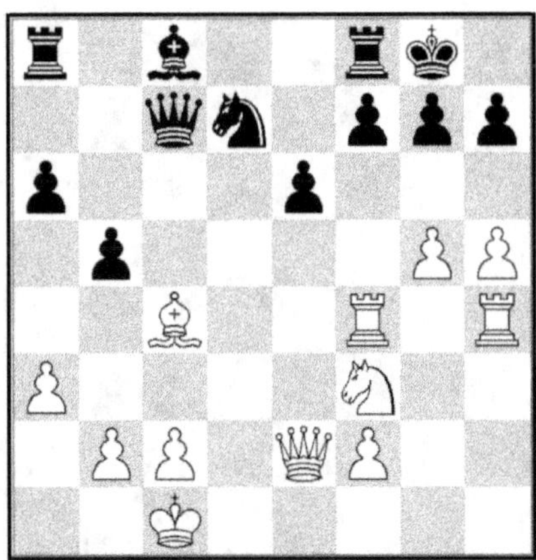

Well, the white Bishop is attacked, and if it retreats, maybe ...♗b7 and who knows... But the white formation is impressive.

96 - White plays ★★

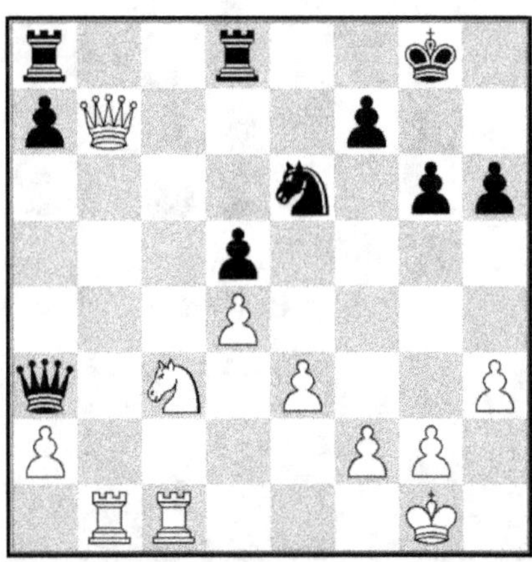

The Black Queen is in some danger, which the Black Queen will use to gain material. How?

4 - The overloaded piece

97 - Black plays ★★

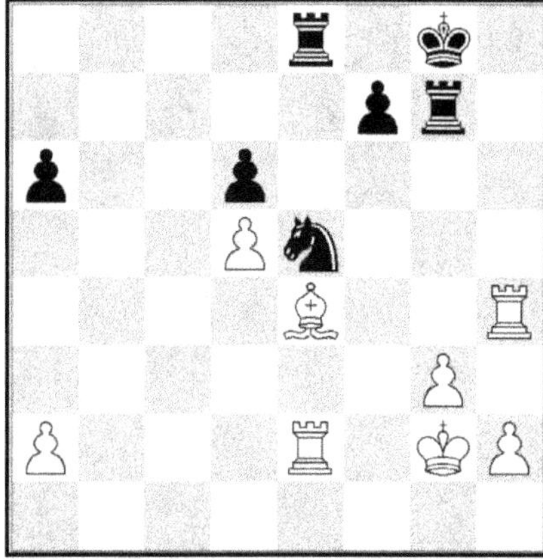

White's last move (**38.♔g2?**) was an important mistake. How can Black exploit it?

99 - White plays ★★

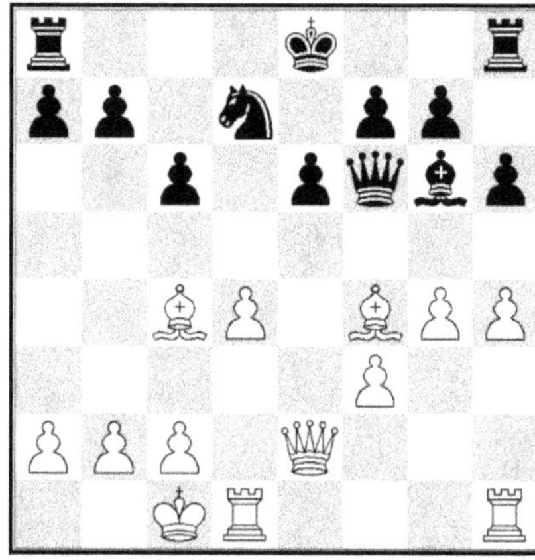

The Black position is unstable and you will find the best way to demonstrate this.

98 - White plays ★★

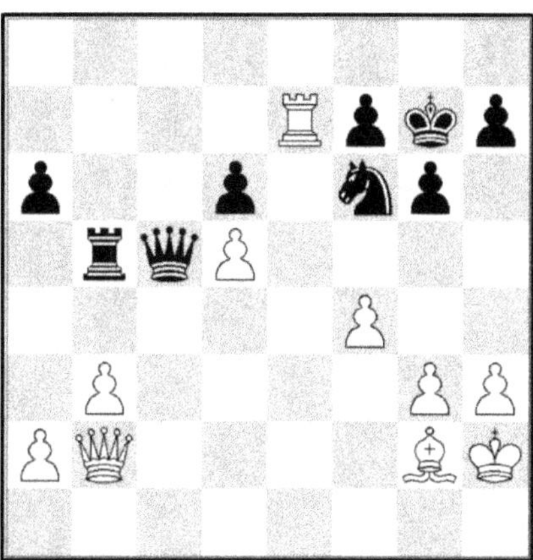

The pin on the large diagonal turns the Knight into a limited piece. Will you be able to take advantage of this?

100 - White plays ★★

Black's development was delayed by the capture of the b-pawn. How could you benefit from this?

4 - The overloaded piece

101 - White plays ★★

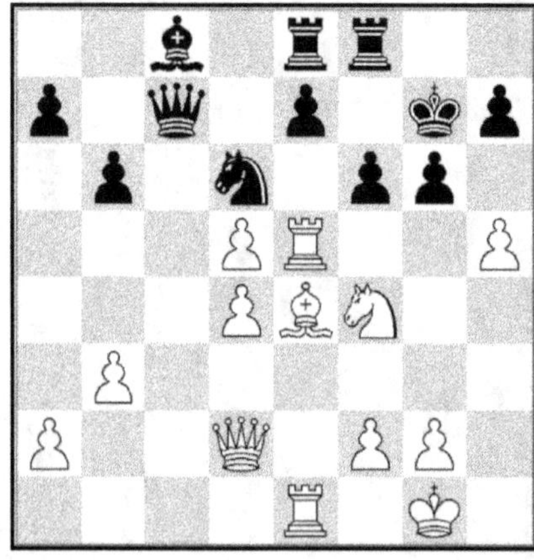

Black has decided that the enemy Rook on e5 is too exposed, attacking it with **25...f6**. Are they right?

103 - White plays ★★

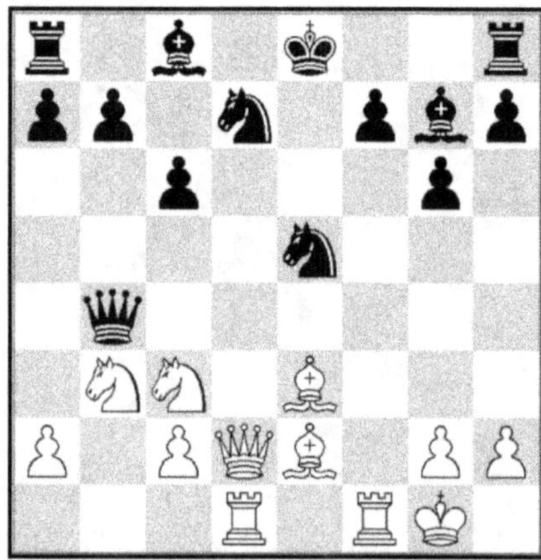

The last move was **14...♞f6–d7** to control c5, but his rival's continuation is unbeatable.

102 - White plays ★★

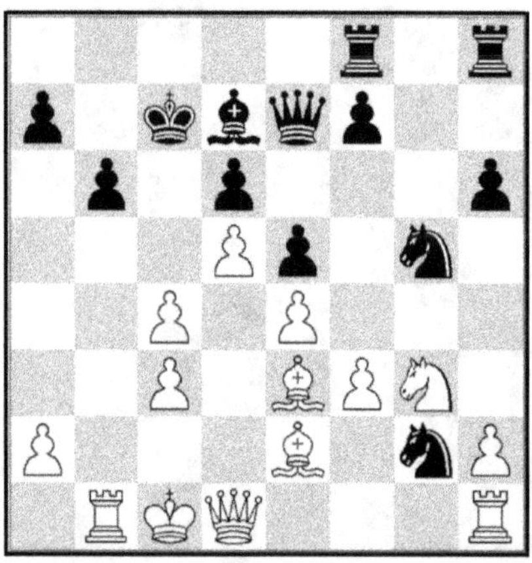

Black has just made a slip (**27...♞h4–g2?**) and will be duly punished for his negligence.

104 - White plays ★★

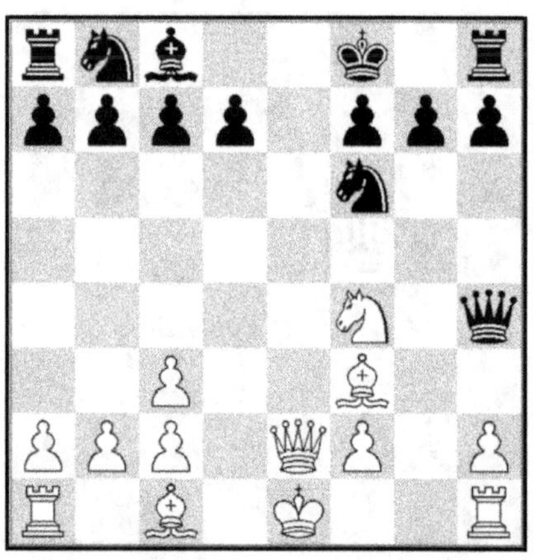

Black has compromised his Queen and his development and White has a very convincing sequence.

4 - The overloaded piece

105 - White plays ★★

The King in the center and the pressure on **d5** don't bode well. How would you proceed?

107 - White plays ★★

In this position of the Philidor Defense there is a winning move, already mentioned by Greco. What is it?

106 - White plays ★★

Black has captured a white pawn on **d7**, but his position is difficult, as his opponent will show.

108 - Black plays ★★

White blundered with **14.♘e2?** (better 14.♗×g5), leaving his position seriously compromised.

4 - The overloaded piece

109 - White plays ★★

The pinned Knight, in connection with other tactical elements, casts a lot of uncertainty over the Black position.

111 - White plays ★★

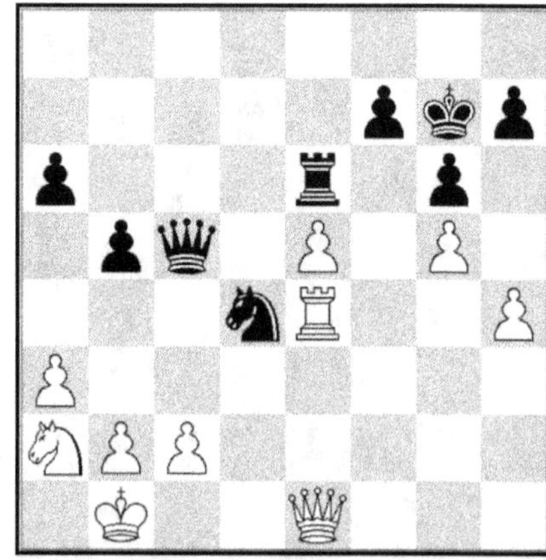

Korchnoi played **30...♘d4**. Does that sound like a good idea? What would your answer be?

110 - White plays ★★

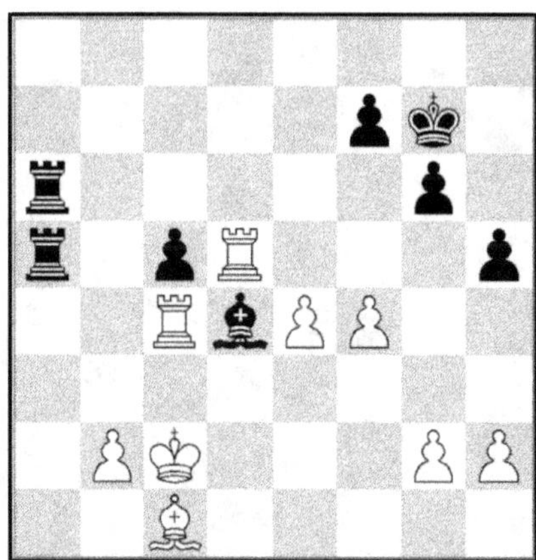

A piece can seem very secure and not really be. Let this position serve as proof.

112 - White plays ★★

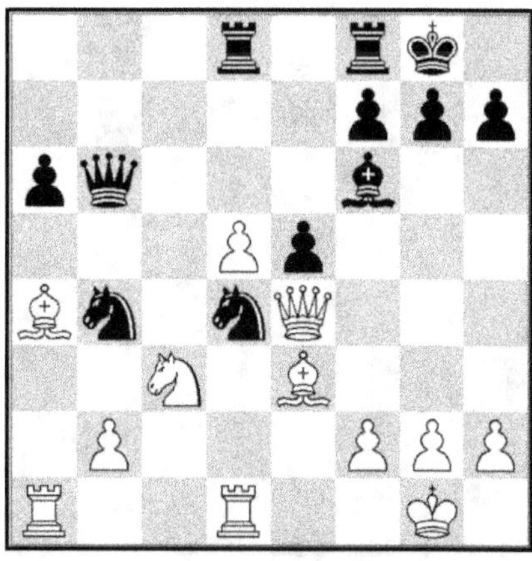

The statement in exercise 110 could also apply to this position, in an even more illustrative way.

4 - The overloaded piece

113 - White plays  ★★★

Optimizing the White game will reveal that there is a compromised piece. How would you proceed?

114 - White plays  ★★★

With very active and well-coordinated pieces, White shouldn't be satisfied with winning a pawn.

115 - White plays  ★★★

In this theoretical position of the Petrov Defense, everything is based on whether a Black piece is finished or not.

116 - Black plays  ★★★

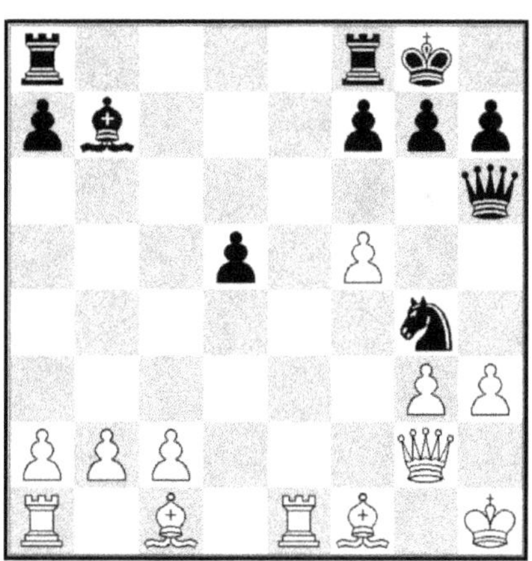

The Knigth is certainly compromised. What direction do you think the game will take?

4 - The overloaded piece

117 - White plays ★★★

In order for some positions to clear up, lines should be opened. It's a way of clearing the fog.

119 - White plays ★★★

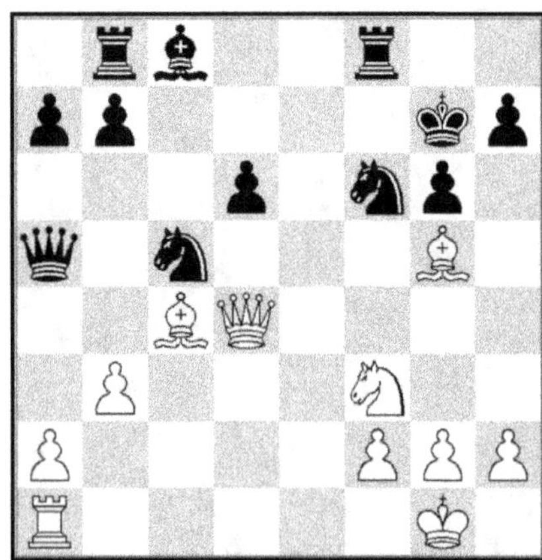

You'll have identified the critical points of the position, but isn't the most problematic thing that White has fewer Rooks?

118 - White plays ★★★

The ♞c6 pin is worrying. But Black is Ivanchuk's game, so he's trying to do well.

120 - White plays ★★★

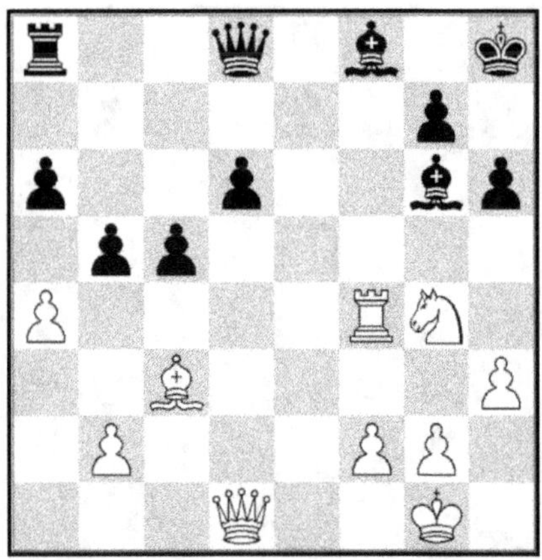

Can the Knight capture on **h6**? Won't it be compromised after, for example, ...♕g5?

4 - The overloaded piece

121 - Black plays ★★★

Black moves into a memorable combination, based on the compromised position of the opposing Queen.

123 - White plays ★★★

29...♘b7 was a serious mistake, after which the Black position collapses. You'll tell us how.

122 - White plays ★★★

I'm asking for something that isn't easy: nothing less than a draw with White!

124 - Black plays ★★★

The great Petrosian's lessons are priceless. Here he masterfully explores the subject that occupies us.

4 - The overloaded piece

125 - White plays ★★★

Black captured a Rook on **d1** and 23.♗×d1 ♘×d1 24.♔×d1 wouldn't be a good deal. Alternatives?

127 - White plays ★★★

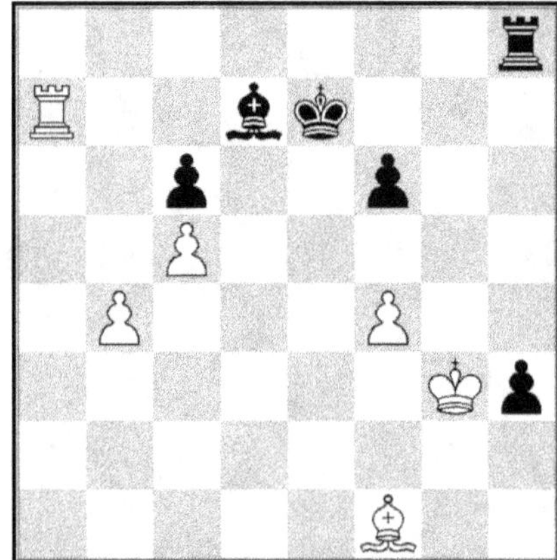

The Black Bishop situation is the key factor in this ending, but winning it requires extreme precision.

126 - White plays ★★★

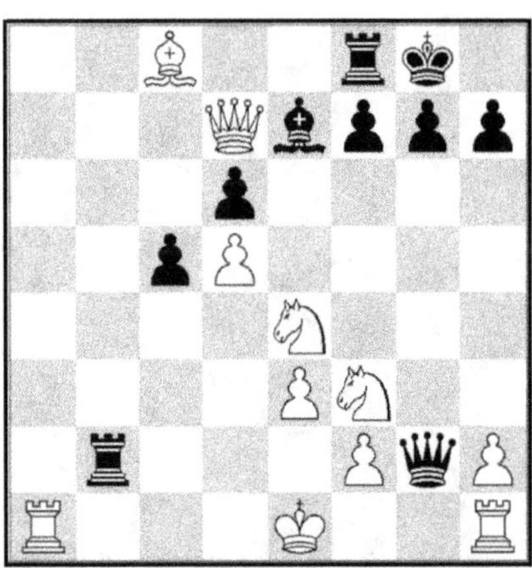

Black has two pieces less, but strong threats. How would you play with White?

128 - White plays ★★★

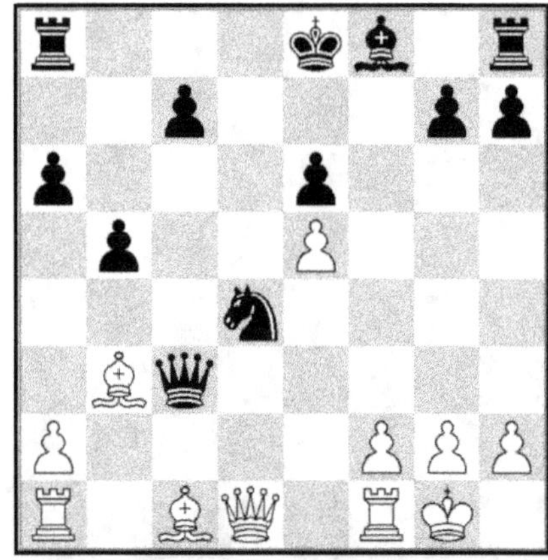

Think freely and emulate Kasparov. If you can do that, you're entitled to be considered an analytical genius.

SOLUTIONS

1 - THE HELPLESS PIECE

1. 9.♕e5+ and 10.♕×b8 (1–0). **Vaulin - Smagin**, Russian Championship, Elista, 1997.

2. 37...♘×d4+ (0–1). **Karaklajic-Zhang Zhong**, Beijing, 1997.

3. 52...♖d2+! (0–1). 53.♔×d2 ♗×a1 54.♘b4 (54.♔c2 ♗c3) 54...♘c3+! **Kacheishvili-Fedorov**, European Country Championship, Leon, 10.11.2001.

4. 45.♘d6+ (1–0). 45...♖e5 46.♘f7+; 45...♔f4 46.♖g4+ ♖e5 47.♘f7+. **Bareev-Onischuk**, Moscow, 2002.

5. 7.♘f3 ♕h5 8.g4! ♕×g4 9.♗×c5 (1–0). **Milov-Castro Acosta**, Sauzal, 2004.

6. 10...♕b4+! 11.♘1d2 (11.♘c3 g5) 11...g5! (0–1). 12.♕×g5 ♗h6. **Smolkin-Matiujin**, Correspondence, 1988.

7. 27...♗×f2+! 28.♖×f2 ♖×c1+ 29.♗×c1 ♖d1+ 30.♔g2 ♖×c1 31.♖×f7? ♖c2+ 32.♖f2 ♕d5+ 33.♔g1 ♖c1+ 34.♖f1 ♖×f1+ 35.♔×f1 ♕h1+ 36.♔f2 ♕×h2+... 51 moves (0–1). **Van Oosterom - Solodovnichenko**, Deizisau, 8.4.2007.

8. 10.♘f4! for if 10...♕×e4+?, 11.♔f2 (threatening ♖e1 and ♗d3) 11.♕c6 12.♕d3! with the double threat of ♗b5 and ♕×h7. Theoretical trap.

9. 34.♕a2 ♔h8 35.♖×d7! ♔×g3+ (35...♔×d7 36.♕a8+ and wins the Rook on f3) 36.h×g3 ♔×d7 37.♕a8+ ♔g7 38.♕e8 (1–0). **C.Balogh-Mamedov**, Moscow (Aeroflot) 15.2.2007.

10. 1.♗h6! ♕f6 (1...♗×h6 2.♕×h6; 1...0–0 2.♗×g7 ♔×g7 3.♕d4+ and 4.♕a7, winning the Rook on b8) 2.♗×g7 ♕×g7 3.♕e3! 1–0. The threat 4.♕a7 has no good defense, because if 3...♖a8, 4.♕a7!! follows anyway 4.♕a7!! (4...♔×a7 5.♔×c8++), and if 3...b6, 4.♕×b6! **Romanovsky-Ravinsky**, Moscow, 1943.

11. 29.♕b3+ ♔f8 30.♖×c3 ♖a3 31.♖f3+ (1–0). **Morozevich-Miton**, Russian Team Championship, Sochi, 2.5.2007.

12. 1.♘g6+! f×g6 2.♖×h7+! ♔×h7 3.♕h3+ ♘h6 4.f×g6+ and 5.♕×d7 (1–0). **Rellstab-Ulrich**, Berlin, 1929.

13. 1...♖d4! 2.♖×d4 c×d4 3.♕×d4 ♖d8! 4.♕c4 ♖c8! 5.♕d4 ♗c5! and the Queen can no longer protect the Bishop. 6.♕c4, 6...♗×e3 etc. (0-1). **Andres-Avrukh**, Spanish Team Championship, Burguillos, 2007.

14. 1.♗×c4! ♕a3 (1...d×c4 2.♕×c4+ ♔h8 3.♕×c6) 2.♗b3 ♕d6 (2...♕×a5 3.♕×c6) 3.♗c7! ♕e6 (3...♕×c7 4.♗×d5+ ♔h8 5.♕×c6) 4.♗×b8 ♖×b8 5.♗a4! ♖×b1 6.♖×b1 ♗×a4 7.♕×a4 ♘c3 8. 8...♕×d7 9.♖b8+ ♔f7 10.♘e5 ♔e7 11.♘×d7. **Kashdan-Tenner**, New York, 1934.

15. 1.♘×e5! d×e5 (1...♕e8 2.♘d3 ♔×e4 3.♘×d6) 2.♕g4, and the double threat on g7 (mate) and d7 (♘h6+, winning the Queen) is decisive **(1-0)**. **Kudrin-Ivkov**, Lone Pine 1981.

16. **40.♕×g5!! f×g5 41.♖×f8 (1–0)**. If 41...♕e7, 42.♖a8 ♘b8 43.♖×a7; if 41...♘b8, 42.♖2f7+ ♖×f7 43.♖×f7+ ♘d7 (43...♔c8?? 44.♗b7++) 44.♖×d7+ ♕×d7 45.♗×d7 ♔×d7 46.h3, with a decisive advantage. **Cebalo-Sulskis**, 3rd European Union Championship, Arvier, 23.6.2007.

2. THE HUNTED OR CLOSED PIECE

17. **1.♔c7 ♘a8+ (1...♘d5+ 2.♔b7) 2.♔b7 (1–0)**. Didactic position.

18. **1.♘b5! ♕×b5 2.♘×c7+** and **3.♘×b5**. A typical pin. Didactic position.

19. **8...b5 (0–1)**. The white Queen is lost. **Lysenko-Voronova**, Frunze, 1978.

20. With **44...♔c3** White loses the Queen. **Short-Lékó**, Sarajevo, 24.5.1999.

21. **17...♘g4! 18.♕f4 g5 (0–1)**. **E.Shneider-Vladimirov**, Svinoujscie, 1978.

22. **7.♘e5 ♗c8?** (7...♘gf6 8.♘×f6+; 7...c6) **8.♗g5**, followed by **♘c6 (1–0)**. **Efremov-Amirjanov**, Kazan, 1981.

23. The capture was bad: **17...♔×a7! ♕×a7 ♗e8!** and the threat of ...♗c5 is definitive (0-1). **Dückstein-Westerinen**, Hamburg, 1968.

24. Yes, if you want to lose the Queen! **8...♕×c2? 9.♗d3**.

25. **17.e×f5 ♖×f5 18.♗a5! ♘c7** (18...♕×a5 19.♕×a5 ♘×a5 20.♗×d7; 18...♘×a5 19.♗×d7 ♖×f3 20.♗×c8) **19.♗×c6 ♗×c6 20.♕×c6 ♘×d5 21.♗×d8 (1–0)**. **Fressinet-Sharbaf**, Turin Olympiad, 23.5.2006.

26. Taking the e6 pawn would be suicide: **19.♕×e6? ♖ae8 20.♕d6 ♕c8**, and the white Queen is hunted down with **21...♔f6**. **Pillsbury-Showalter**, Nuremberg, 5.8.1896.

27. **11.♕a4! ♗d7 12.♗a5 ♕a6** (12...♗×b5 13.c×b5) **13.♘c7+ ♔f8 14.♕a3 (1–0)**. **Robatsch-S.García**, Sochi, 1974.

28. **8.♗g5! ♗×f3 9.♕d2!** winning the Queen. This trick is worth knowing. It occurs in Rubinstein's French, after **1.e4 e6 2.d4 d5 3.♘d2(c3) d×e4 4.♘×e4 ♗d7 5.♘f3 ♗c6 6.♗d3 ♘f6 7.♘×f6+ ♕×f6**. Tarrasch mentioned this in his game with Mieses (Berlin, 1916), but more than one prominent player has fallen into this trap, for example in the games Kotkov-Akopian (Krasnodar, 1966) and Suetin - Zilberman (Kirovobad, 1973).

29. **1.♘d5** (1.♔×a8? ♔c7 2.♘d5+ ♔c8 and the white King can't get out of the cage) **1...♔d8 2.♘b6 ♘c7 3.♔c6!**. *Zugzwang*. The black Khight falls **(1-0)**. Didactic position.

30. The relatively best is 15...♕×a3 16.♗×b5+ ♘c6 17.♖b3 ♕a2 18.0-0, but in the match it was played **15...♕×d4? 16.♗×b5+ ♔d8 17.c3 (1–0)**. **Lutikov-Gavrikov**, Moscow, 1972.

31. **14.♘c4! ♕×d4** (14...♕c7 15.♖×e7) **15.♗e3 (1–0)**. **Aseev-Svedchikov**, Moscow, 1994.

32. **38...♖h7! 39.♕e5 ♕c8 40.♕f4 ♔f8 41.♕e5 ♔f5 (0–1)**. **Bobotsov-**

Petrosian, Lugano Olympiad, 26.10.1968.

33. 22.g3 Rh5 23.Bd1 Rg5 24.h4 Rg6 25.h5 Rg5 26.e4 R×h5 27.B×h5 N×h5 28.Qd3 Bc5 29.Rac1 Ra8 30.Rc2 Ndf6 31.Rfc1 Rd8 32.Qf3 N×g3... 41 moves **(1–0)**. **Dreev-Jenkin**, Saint-Vincent, 24.9.2006.

34. 9.Na4! Q×a2 10.Bc4 Bg4 (10...Qa3 11.Kc3) **11.Nf3 B×f3 12.g×f3! (1–0)**. 12...Qa3 13.Rc3 Nc2+(d3+) and Black saves the Queen, but loses a piece, with a catastrophic position. **Botvinnik-Spielmann**, Moscow, 15.2.1935.

35. 1.Kh6 Kh8 2.Nh4 Kg8 3.Nf3 Kh8 4.Ne5 Kg8 5.Nc6 Kh8 6.Ne7 **(1–0)**. Study by **A. Troitzky**, *Novoe Vremia*, 1898.

36. The move is a mistake. White should have played 25.K×d8+ N×d8, even though Black had an advantage. After 25...Kf8! K×e6 is not possible, as 26...Kf7, gaining quality. **26.B×c5 N×c5 27.R×c7 Ne6 28.Ra7 B×f3 29.K×f3 Rc8 30.g4 R×c3+ 31.Ke2 f×g4 32.f5 g×h3 33.Ra8+ Ke7 (0–1)**. **Darga-Ivkov**, Hastings, 1955-56.

37. 1.Qe4! f5 2.Q×a8 Nbc6 3.Bf4! Qd7 4.Bb5 Bb7 (4...Ba6 5.Q×f8+ K×f8 6.B×a6) **5.Q×a7! (1–0)**. Didactic position.

38. 12.b×c3! Q×c3+ 13.Qd2 Q×a1 14.Bb1! **(1–0)**. There's no defense against 15.Bb2, which wins the Queen. **Nezhmetdinov - Konstantinov**, Rostov, 1936.

39. 1.Rb6! Kh7 (1...Kf7 2.Rh6! Kg7 3.Rh3 Ne2 4.Kf5) 2.Kf6 Kh6 3.Rb2! Nh5+ 4.Kf7 g4 (4...Ng3 5.Rh2+ Nh5 6.Rh1) 5.f×g4 Ng3 6.Rb5 **(1–0)**. **Rogers-Antic**, Adelaide,

2007.

40. 12...Nd5+! 13.Bd2 Qb6! (13...Qd8? 14.Q×c6+ Qd7 15.Q×a8+) **14.Q×a8+ Kd7 15.0-0** (15.a4 Nc7 16.a5 Q×b2) **15...Nc7 16.Ba5 N×a8 17.B×b6 N×b6** Nxb6 ...36 moves. **(0–1)**, **Nimzovich-Alekhine**, Bled, 17.9.1931.

41. 1.f6! (1.B×a4 B×a4 2.K×a4 Ke7 −+) **1...Nb2** (1...Nb6 2.Kc5 Nc8 3.Bd7 Na7 4.Kb6) **2.Kc3 Ba4! 3.Bf3! Nd1+ 4.Kd2 Nf2 5.Ke3 Nh3 6.Bg4 Ng1 7.Kf2** and the Knight falls. Draw. Study by **G. Kasparian** (1949).

42. 13.R×e5! B×e5 14.Ne4 B×h2+ (14...Q×d5 15.N×e5+ Kc8 16.Q×d5 N×d5 17.N×f7, with a clear advantage) **15.N×h2 Qe5 16.Ng4 Qf5** (16...Qg7 17.Nef6+ Kc8 18.Bh6) **17.Ngf6+ Kc8 18.g4! Qe5 19.f4 (1–0)**. **Tikhomirov-Sliusarev**, Moscow, 1980.

43. 20.g5! h5 (20...Q×f4 21.Rdf1 Qh4 22.Rg4 Qh3 23.g×h6 Q×h6 24.Rfg1 Rfd8 25.Qf2) **21.Qe3 g6** (21...Q×h2 22.Rg3 Rfd8 23.Rdg1) **22.Rg3 Rad8 23.Rdg1 (1–0)**. **Sadvakasov-Wu Wenjin**, Asian Individual Championship, 15.10.2005.

44. 15.Nb3! N×f2+ 16.Ke1! (16.Q×f2 Q×b3+ 17.Kc1 Rd8 18.Qe1 e5) **16...N×h1 17.Qc3! (1–0)**. If 17...f6, 18.N×c5, and the black Queen wins. **Karpov-Korchnoi**, Odessa (fast), 31.5.2008.

45. 23.Bf2! Q×a4 24.Bd1 Bb3 25.B×b3 **(1–0)**. 25...Qb4 26.B×f7+ R×f7 27.R×b4 B×b4 28.Ke2. **Golod-Mikhalevski**, Israel Team Championship, 21.1.2006.

46. 24.g4 Rd5 25.Ba2! Rb5 26.b4 a5 27.Nc3! a×b4 28.N×b5 c×b5

29.Rde1 R×a3 30.B×e6+ Q×e6 31. Qc4? (31...Q×g4+!! 32.h×g4 b×a3 33.Rb1 Bb6 34.Rfd1 N×g4 35.Rd3) 32.Qe3 Bb6 33.Rd1 b3 34.g5 Nd5 35.Qe8+ (1–0). **Govciyan-Mokry**, Issy-les-Moulineaux, 25.5.2006.

47. 25.Ba4 Qe6 26.Bd7 Qd6 (26...Qg6 27.N×d5!) 27.Rc6 R×d7 28.R×d6 R×d6 29.f3 Nf6 30.e4 Bg6 31.e5 Rc6 32.Rf1...48 moves. (1–0). **Ernst-Lputian**, European Club Cup, 9.10.2006.

48. 54...N×d4 55.N×g6 Nc6! 56.Re2 Re6 57.Nf8+ Re7 58.Nh7 Kf7, and the white Knight falls after ...Kg7 (0–1). **Ivanchuk-Shirov**, Calzada de Calatrava (fast), 8.4.2007.

3. THE RESTRICTED OR OFFSIDE PIECE

49. The best answer would be 1...Re8!, and if 2.Rf1 (2.R×e8 N×e8), 2...Ng8. 2.Re4! and there is no satisfactory answer against 3.Rh4+ (1–0). **L.Steiner-Tartakower**, Budapest, 1928.

50. 10.Nf5! B×f5 11.e×f5 (the Bishop blockade on g7 is accentuated) 11...Qa5 12.Qf4 Kc8 13.Kb1 Kg8 14.Bc4 Qe5 (14...Kf8) 15.Qf3 Qc5 (15...Nd4 16.Q×b7 R×c4 17.Rhe1) 16. Bb3 Rc7 17.Rhe1 Rd7 (17...Nd4 18.Ba4+ Kd8 19.Qd5) 18.Qh5 Nd8 19.Re3 Rf8 20.Rd5 Qc7 21.Rd4 Qa5 22.Ra4 Qb6 23.Be6 N×e6 24.f×e6 Rc7 25.e×f7+ (1–0). hombrexlobo-slesicki, Internet, 2009.

51. 23.Qf3! Qe6? (23...Rg7 24.Q×d5 Rgd8 25.Qe4 Qe6 26.f4!) 24.Qf6! Qc8 (24...Q×f6 25.e×f6 Ke8 26.R×b5; 24...g5 25.R×b5 Rg6 26.Qh8+! Kg8 27.Q×h7 Geller)

25.f4! Qb7 26.Ra5 Ke8 27.Rba1 b4 28.c×b4 Q×b4 29.R×d5 Qb7 30.e6 (1–0). **Geller–Unzicker**, Saltsjöbaden Interzonal, 22.9.1952.

52. 23...Bc7 24.g3 B×g3 25.Re2 Bd3 26.Rg2 Be4 27.Qh6 Qf6 28.B×c4 Qf2 (0–1). **Obodchuk-Sutovsky**, Turin Olympiad, 21.5.2006.

53. 48...Ne4! 49.h×g5 (49...B×e4? K×e4 50.h×g5 h×g5 51.K×g5 K×e3) 49...h×g5 50.Bb1 (50.Bd3 Nf2+; 50.Kf3 Nc3 51.Kg4 Kf6; 50. Kh5 N×g3+ 51.K×g5 Nf1 Rublevsky) 50...Nc3 51.Bc2 Kf6 52.Kh5 N×a2 53.e4 d4 54.e5+ K×e5 55.K×g5 Nc1 56.g4 d3 57.Bd1 a4 (0–1). **Issabayev-Rublevsky**, Turin Olympiad, 21.5.2006.

54. 47.Rg7+! Ke8 (47...Q×g7 48.Nh5+; 47...K×g7 48.Nh5+; 47...Kf8 48.Ne6+) 48.Qg3 Qf5 49.Rg5 (49.Nh5! Q×h5 50.Qc7, and mate) 49...Qf6 50.Nh5 Qd4 51.Rg7 c3 52.R×h7 Bb3 53.Qg6+ Kf8 54.Qh6+ Kg8 55.Rg7+ (1–0). **Moradiabadi - Le Quang**, Turin Olympiad, 25.5.2006.

55. 25.Nd2 Nd3 26.Rf1 Raf8 (26...Nge5 27.b3) 27.N×e4 N×b2 28.N×d6 R5f6 29.Rb3 R×d6 30.R×b2 b6 31.Nf3 Rd7 32.Rfb1 Re8 33.a5 b5 34. c×b5 a×b5 35.R×b5 R×d5 36.Rb7 e7 37.a6 Rd6 38.R×e7 N×e7 39.Rb7 Nc6 40.Nd2 Rd3 41.Rc7 Rd6 42.g4 e6 43.Kg2 g5 44.Nc4 Kf8 45.Na3 (1–0). If 45...Bb8, 46.Rc8+ Kf7 47.R×b8 N×b8 48.a7. **Areshchenko-Johannessen**, Bundesliga, 25.2.2007.

56. 1.Ne4! N×d5 (1...f×e4? 2.I×e4; 1...Qe8 2.Nf4 De Dovitiis) 2.Ng5 Nf6 3.Ng3. The threat 4.Nh5 is unstoppable (1–0). **Flores-Orsini**. Avellaneda, 2007.

57. 23.Qd6! Q×d6 (23...Ra1+

24.Kb2 Q×d6 25.R×d6 Rh1 26.Bg3)
24.R×d6 Ra4 25.B×f6 R×c4+ 26.Kd2
g×f6 27.Nc3! Rb4 28.R×b6 Ba8
29.Ra6 Bb7 30.Ra7 (1–0). **Ernst-Rau**, Bundesliga, 10.12.2005.

58. 33.Bh5+! K×h5 (33...Kf5
34.Qd6! e5 35.f3; 33...Kg7 34.Q×f7+
Kh8 35.Q×f6+ Kg8 36.Bf7+ Kh7
37.Qg6+ Kh8 38.Q×h6++)
34.Q×f7+ Kg4 35.Qg6++ (1–0).
H.Olafsson-Rodgaard, Munkebo
Zonal, 12.9.1998.

59. 16.N×b7 Q×b7 17.Qd5+!
Q×d5 18.N×d5 Nc5 19.B×c5 d×c5
(successive exchanges accentuate
White's advantage) 20.e×f5 B×b2
21.N×e7+ Kh8 22.f6 Bc3+ 23. Kf1
Bd2 24.Rg1 Rab8 25.Rgg4 Rb1+
26.Kf2 Rh1 27.Kg2 Rc1 28.Bd3 Rd8
29.Rae4 a5 30.Nc6 Rf8 31.Ne5 c4
32.R×c4 Be3 33.Nd7 (1–0). **Al
Modiahki-Williams**, Amsterdam,
21.7.2005.

60. 9...N×c3! 10.B×c6+ b×c6
11.Q×c6+ Bd7 12.Q×a8+? (12.Re1+
Kd8 13.Q×a8+ Bc8 14.d4! B×d4
15.Be3) 12...Ke7 13.Q×h8 (13.Qf3)
13...Ne2+ 14.Kh1 B×f2 15.h3
Q×h3+! 16.g×h3 Bc6+ 17.Kh2
Bg3++. **Amateur-Tarrasch**, Munich,
1932.

61. 11...Nd5! (blocks the Queen's
return along the long diagonal)
12.Rd1? (12.B×d5 Kb8 13.Qa6
e×d5) 12...Kb8 13.Qc6 Qh4! 14.
15.Q×d7 N×f4! 16.Ne2 (16.e×f4??
Q×f2+ 17.Kh1 Qf3++) 16...Nh3+
17.Kg2 N×f2 18.Rd4 (18.Rf1 Ng4
19.h3 Ne5) 18...Ng4 19.Rf4 Q×h2+
20.Kf1 B×e3 21.Bd5 B×f4 (0–1).
Foguelman-Bronstein, Amsterdam
Interzonal, 1964.

62. 15.f×e7! b×a1=Q 16.R×a1
K×e7? (16...Qc5 17.Qg3 Q×e7
18.Q×g7 Rf8 19.Rb1) 17.Rb1 Bc8
18.Qg3 Kf8 (18...Qc5 19.Be3 Qd5
20. Q×g7 Kf8 21.Be4! Q×e4
22.Bc5+) 19.Bd6+ Kg8 20.Be5 g6
21.Qg5 h6 22.Qf6 Rh7 23.B×g6!
f×g6 24.Q×g6+ Kf8 25.Bd6+ (1–0).
25...Re7 26.Qf6+ Kg8 27.Q×e7.
Anand-Morovic, São Paulo, 22.8.2004.

63. 25...c5!! 26.N×g5 Bd5! (the
Bishop supports e6, the crux of the
position) 27.Nf3 (27.N×e6!? B×e6
28.b×c5) 27...c×b4 28.a×b5 a×b5
29.Nh4 Qg5, with a decisive advantage. **Kramnik-Anand**, Belgrade, 1997.

64. 25.Nd3 Nc6?! (25...R×c1)
26.Nc5 Qe7 27.N×b7! N×d4
28.R×c7 R×c7 29.Nc5 R×c5 30.Q×d4
Rc6 31.b5 a×b5 32.a6 Rc8 33.Qb6!
(33.a7 Qb7) 33...Qf8 34.a7 (1–0).
Pelletier-Sebag, French Team
Championship, 30.4.2007.

65. 23.c4! N×c4 24.Nf3! Na5
25.Rh4! Bg7 (25...c4 26.B×g6! f×g6
27.Q×g6 h×g6 28.Rh8+ Kf7
29.Ng5++) 26.Be4 Qd7 (26...Qb3
27.Qd2!) 27.B×g7 B×e4 28.Qc1!
B×f3 29.Qh6 f5 30.Q×h7+ Kf7
31.g×f3 Kg8 32.Bf8+! (1–0).
Sutovsky-Miton, Montreal, 28.7.2007.

66. 16.Ng2 Nd5 17.Nf4 0-0-0
18.Rfe1 N×f4?! 19.B×f4 Bd6
20.R×d6 Q×d6 21.Re5 Kb8 22.Rc4
Rhe8 23.Rae1! Re7 24.b4 Rc7?!
(24...Rde8 25.Qf4 f6! 26.R×e6 Q×f4
27.g×f4 R×e6 28.R×e6 Rg8!) 25.h4 h5
26.a4 Qf8 27.Qf4 Rdc8 28.Bf1! Bh7
29.Be2 Bg6 30.Bf3 Ka8 31.b5 Qa3
32.a5! c×b5 33.R×b5 a6 34.R×b7
R×b7 35.Rb1 Qe7 (35...Rbc8
36.Qc7) 36.R×b7 Q×b7 37.B×b7+
K×b7 38.Qd6 Rc6 39.Qb4+ Kc8
40.f4 (1–0). **Grischuk-Bauer**, French
Team Championship, 7.5.2005.

67. 23.g4! f×g4 24.♘g5 ♘f6 25.♘g3 ♖c7 26.♕d3 g×h3 27.♘5e4 (27.♘×h7 e4) 27...♗g4 28.♗g5 c4 29.♕e3 ♖f7 30.f3 ♗c8 31.♘h5 ♘×d5 32.♕d2 ♘e7 (32...♘f6 33. ♘e×f6+ ♗×f6 34.♘×f6+♖×f6 35.♔h2 ♖ef8 36.♖g1) 33.♔h1 ♖ef8 34.♖g1 ♗f5 35.♗f6 ♗g6 36.♗×g7 ♖×g7 37.♘hg6?! (37.♕h6! Kovalev) 37...♖×f6 38.♘×f6+... 48 moves (1-0). **Kovalev - Zilberman**, Oberwart, 10.7.2007.

68. 19.♕×f7+! (19.e×d4 ♕e7) 19...♖h8 20.e×d4 ♖e7 21.♕h5 g6 22.♕h6 ♖g7 23.♗a3 ♘e6 24.♖f6 ♕e8 (24...♘×d4 25.♖ef1 c5 26. ♖×g6 ♖×g6 27.♗×g6 ♕g8 28.♗h5) 25.♖ef1 c5 26.d×c5 b×c5 27.♕h3 ♗c8 28.♗c1 ♔g8 29.♗h6 ♖e7 30.♕f3 ♗b7 31.♗b5 (1-0). Shengelia-Weiss, Traunsee, 2007.

69. 36.f6! (36.♖e6? ♘c5 37.♖×a6 ♘×a6 38.♗b7 ♖c5 39.♗×a6 ♖a5 40.♗b7 ♖×a3, advantage for Black - Beliavsky) 36...g×f6 37.♖e6 ♘c5 38.♖×f6+ ♔g7 39.♖f5 ♘b3 40.♗d5 ♖c7 41.♖g5+ ♔f6 42.♖g4 ♘d2 43.♖d4 ♘b3 44.♖h4 ♔g7 45.♗e4 ♔h8 (45...h6 46. ♖g4+ ♔f8 47.♖g6 Beliavsky) 46.♗d5 ♔g7 47.♔g2 ♘d2 48.♖d4 ♘b3 49.♖g4+ ♔f6 50.♖f4+ ♔g7 51.h4 ♘c1 52.♖g4+ ♔f8 53. ♖g8+ ♔e7 54.♗e4 ♔d6 55.♖g5 ♖f7 56.♖d5+ ♔e7 57.♗e4 ♔d6 58.♖g5 ♖f7 59.♖d5+ ♔c7 60.♖c5+ ♔d8 61.f3 ♖d7 62.g4 (1-0). **Beliavsky-Khalifman**, Bazna, 25.6.2007.

70. 24.♖cf1! ♖×e4 25.f×g6! f6 (25...♖×f4?? 26.g×h7++; 25...♕×g6 26.♕×f7+ ♕×f7 27.♖×f7) 26.♕g5! ♕d7 27.♔g1!! (27.♖×f6 ♗×f6 28.♕×f6 h×g6 29.♕×g6+ ♔h8 30.♗g5 ♖4e6! 31.♗f6+ ♖×f6 32.♕×f6+ ♕g7 33.♕h4+ ♔g8 Geller) 27...♗g7 28.♖×f6 ♖g4 (28...♗×f6

29.♕×f6 h×g6 30.♕×g6+ ♔h8 31.♗g5 ♖4e6 32.♗f6+ ♖×f6 33.♖×f6! Geller) 29.g×h7+ ♔h8 30.♗×g7+ ♕×g7 31.♕×g4! (1-0). 31...♕×g4 32.♖f8+ ♖×f8 33.♖×f8+. **Geller-Smyslov**, Candidates (5th), Moscow, 1965.

71. 22...♖g6! 23.g3 (23.♗f3 ♗×f3 24.♖×d8 ♖×g2+ 25.♔f1 ♖×h2 26.♖×f8+ ♗×f8; 23.♗f1 ♗×b4 24.♖e3 ♗c5 25.♖g3 ♕f6 26. ♕e2 ♗b7 Ftacnik) 23...♗×b4 24.♗c4 ♗×e1 25.♗×d5 (25.♖×d5 ♕f6) 25...♕e7 26.a4 ♖f6 27.f4 ♕e3+ 28.♔h1 ♗×g3! (0-1). 29.h×g3 ♕f2! **Ivanchuk-Anand**, Wijk aan Zee, 16.1.2006.

72. 36.f4! ♖×c3 37.h5! g×h5 38.♖f8 ♖a3 39.f5! ♗×f5 40.♖×f7+ ♔g8 41.♖g7+ ♔f8 42.♖b7 ♖a8 43.♔g3! ♖d8 44.♔f4 ♗e4 45.g3 c3 46.♖f7+ ♔g8 47.♖g7+ ♔f8 48.♘d7+ ♖×d7 (48...♔e8?? 49.♖e7++) 49.♖×d7 (1-0). **Carlsen-Aronian**, Candidates (5th), Elista, 2007.

73. 24.♖d3! h4 25.♖h3 ♗d8 26.♔a2! ♔f8 (26...d5 27.♕g4 d4 28.♘b1) 27.♕e1 ♗e8 28.♖×h4 ♖×h4 29.♕×h4 ♕g1 30.♕h8+ ♖e7 31.h4 d5 32.e×d5 ♕×g2 33.h5 (1-0). **Lékó-Morozevich**, World Championship, Mexico, 28.9.2007.

74. 17.c6! b6 (17...b×c6 18.♗c5; 17...♕e8 18.♗c5 ♔f7 19.h4, winning the Knight) 18.b5 a6 19.a4 a×b5? (19...a5) 20.a×b5 ♔×a1 21.♕×a1 ♘f7 22. ♕c3 ♕h4 23.♖a1 ♘g5 24.♕e1 ♕h5 25.♖a7 ♕g6 26.♔h1 (26.♖×c7? ♘×f3) 26...♕h5 27.f4 ♘e4 28.♖×c7 g5 29.♗×b6 ♔h8 30.♗×e4 f×e4 31.♗c5 ♖g8 (1-0). Then 32.♗e7. **Petrosian-Fischer**, Candidates Tournament, Yugoslavia, 1959.

75. 30.♘g5 ♖ff8 31.♖e2 ♗g7 32.♕c2 ♖de8 33.♘e3! ♗h6 34.♗d5

♗g7 (34...♗×g5 35.h×g5, to continue with f4) **35.♕d1 h6 36.♘e4 ♕d8 37.♖a2 ♗c8 38.♘c3! h5 39.♗e4 ♖e6 40.♘cd5 ♗h6 41.♘g2 ♔g7?! 42.f4 e×f4 43.♘g×f4 ♖e5 44.♘×g6! ♔×f1 45.♕×f1 ♖×e4 46.d×e4 ♔×g6 47.♖f2 ♕e8** (47...♗g7 48.♖f7) **48.e5! d×e5** (48...♕×e5 49.♖e2) **49.♖f6+ ♔g7 50.♖d6 (1-0)**. **Kasparov-Karpov**, World Championship (8th), Seville, 2.11.1987.

76. **23.c3! f5 24.♖b1 ♗a3 25.♖b5 ♕c6 26.♕g3 ♗d7** (26...f4 27.♕×f4 ♗d6 28.♕h4+ ♔f7 29.♖f5+ g×f5 30.♗×c6; 26...♗d6 27.♘×f5+ g×f5 28.♕g7+ ♔d8 29.♖b4) **27.♘×f5+! ♔d8** (27...g×f5 28.♕g7+ ♔d8 29.♕×h8+ ♔c7 30.♕×a8) **28.♖b4 ♕c7 29.♕h4+ ♔c8 30.♗×d7+ ♔×d7 31.♕e7+ (1-0)**. 31...♔c8 32.♘d6+. **Gashimov-Tiviakov**, Reggio Emilia, 4.1.2008.

77. **21.e5! d×e5 22.♘de4 ♕f5** (22...♘×d5 23.♘c5; 22...♗f8 23.f×e5 ♖×e5 24.♘f6+ ♘×f6 25.♖×e5) **23.♕f2 ♖ad8** (23...♗f8 24.♕b6 ♕×f4 25.♗g3) **24.♗×d8 ♖×d8 25. ♕b6 ♕c8 26.♘c5 e4** (26...♘a8 27.♕a7; 26...♗a8 27.d6! ♗×f3 28.d×c7 ♖f8 29.♖d8 ♕f5 30.c8♕) **27.♕×b7 e×f3 28.♕×c8 ♖×c8 29.d6 ♗f8 30.♘b7 ♘e6 31.d7 ♖b8 32.♖×e6 (1-0)**. Petrosian-Larsen, Palma de Mallorca, 1968.

78. **25...f3+ 26.g×f3 ♘f4+ 27.♔e3 ♖f6 28.♗×e7? ♘g2+ 29.♔e2 ♖×f3 30.♗d6** (30.♗g5? ♖bf8 31.♖f1 ♘g4) **30...♘f4+ 31. 32.♖d2 ♖e8 33.♘c4** (one of the white Knights is activated) **33...♘×h2+ 34.♔g1 ♘g4 35.♖f1?!** (35.♗c5 h5! "and White's position is untenable" Stohl) **35...♗d4 36.♗c5 ♖g3+ 37.♔h1 ♖h3+ 38.♔g1 ♘h2 (0-1)**. **Hübner-Kasparov**, Brussels, 1986.

79. **21.b4! ♘d7** (21...c×b4 22.♗×b4 ♖fd8 23.c5 d×c5 24.♗×c5 Kharitonov) **22.b5! a×b5 23.♖a7 ♖fc8 24.♗a5! ♘b6** (24...♘a8 25.c×b5 ♘ab6 26.♗×b6! ♖×b6 27.♘c4 Kharitonov) **25.c×b5 ♕d7 26.♔g2! c4 27.♗×b6 ♖×b6 28.♘×c4 ♖×b5 29.♘b6 ♖×b6 30.♖×b6 ♗f6 31.♘f3 ♗e7 32.♖c6 ♗d8 33.♘d2 ♕e8 34.♘c4 (1-0)**. **Petrosian-Hort**, Wijk aan Zee, 1971.

80. **29.♘×g6 ♕×g6 30.♕c3 ♔h7?** (30...♕f7) **31.♗f4 ♕f7 32.♗e5 ♕d7 33.h4 ♔g8 34.h5 ♕d8 35.♕g3 ♕d7 36.♗d6 ♕f7 37.♗e5 ♕f5 38.♕e2 b4 39. g4 ♕f6 40.♗e5 ♕g5 41.♔g2 b3 42.♗d6 ♔f7 43.♕d1 ♔g8 44.♗g3 ♕f6** (44...♘b4 45.♕×b3 ♕e7 46.♕a4) **45.♗e5 ♕h4 46.♗g3 ♕f6 47.♕d2! ♕e7 48.♕e3 ♕f6 49.♗d6! ♔h7 50.♕×b3 ♕×d4 51.♕c2+ ♔h8** (51...♕e4+ 52.♕×e4+ d×e4 53.b4) **52.♕c8+ ♔h7 53.♕c2+ ♔h8 54.♕c8+ ♔h7 55.♕×e6 ♕×b2** (55...♘c5 56.♕f5+ ♔g8 57.♕c8+ ♔h7 58.♗×c5) **56.♗e5 ♕c2 57.♕e7 ♕e4+ 58.♔g3 (1-0)**. **Gelfand-Lautier**, Horgen, 1994.

4 - THE OVERLOADED PIECE

81. **26...♗f8 27.♕f2 ♗×b4 (0-1)**. **Cebalo - Fercec**, Croatian Championship 1998.

82. **22.♘d5+! (1-0)**. 22...e×d5 23.♕×c7+, winning the Queen. **Vescovi-Karpov**, São Paulo (fast), 2004.

83. **58...♖d4+ 59.♖f5 ♖b5+ (0-1)**. 60.♔f6 (60 ♖e6 ♖d6+) 60...♖d6+ 61.♖e6 ♖h6+ and the Rook falls on e6. **Van der Weide-I.Sokolov**, Dutch

Championship, 1998.

84. **1.f4! K×f4 2.R×g7+ K×g7 3.R×g5+** and **4.K×f4 (1–0)**. Didactic position.

85. **28.Q×e6! (1–0)**. 28...R×e6 29.N f7+ Kg8 30.N×d8 Rf6 31.Ke2 Rd6 32.Nb7 Re6+ 33.Kd3 Rf6 34.Ne5. **Smirin-Pelletier**, Biel, 28.7.2002.

86. **7.Rb1 Qa3 8.Nb2 Q×a2** (8...Qa6?? 9.N×c7) **9.N×c7+ Kd8 10.N×a8**. The theoretical move is 6...c6.

87. **1.Nb5!** (1.Nd5! Qa5 2.Qa3) **1...Qa5** (1...Q×f3?? 2.Nc7++) **2. 2...Qb6 3.N×d6+ B×d6 4.Q×d6+**. **Rogoff-Bertok**, Sarajevo, 1971.

88. **9.Ne5! Bg6** (9...e6? 10.N×f7 K×f7 11.Q×e6+ Kg6 12.Qf7+ Kf5 13.Be6++) **10.h4! h5 11.N×g6 f×g6 12.Qd3**, with a clear advantage. Scandinavian defense line.

89. **1.Re8!!** (1.Rh8+? K×h8 2.d8Q+ Kg7; 1.e6 Rg7 2.Rc8 Ra1; 1.Rc8 R×d7 2.e6 Rd8! 3.R×d8 Rf6) **1...R×d7 2.e6 (1–0)**. Study by **G. Kasparian** (1940).

90. **1...Nfg4!** (threatens to win the Queen with 2...Bg5) **2.b4** (2.h4 g5!) **2...Qb6 3.Nd5 e×d5 4.e×d5 Bg5 5.Qe4 Nf6**, with Rook advantage without compensation **(0-1)**. 6.Qe2 B×d2 7.Q×d2. **Fichtl-Sajtar**, Prague, 1943.

91. **9...N×f4 10.N×f4 Be3! (0–1)**. 11.Q×e3 N×c2+ and 12...N×e3. **Badev-Filev**, Sofia, 15.5.2006.

92. **8...R×h2! 9.R×h2 Qa5+! 10.c3** (10.Qd2) **10...Q×e5+!! 11.d×e5 g×h2**, and a new Queen on g1 or h1, with a piece advantage. **Schuster-Carls**, Bremen, 1914.

93. **1.c7 Nb7 2.c8N!!** (2.c8=Q? Nd6+) **2...B×c8** (2...K×g6 =) **3.Kb6! Nd6 4.Kc7**. Draw. Study by **A. Troitzky** (1922).

94. **1.B×e6! f×e6** (1...Nc5 2.B×f7+; 1...Bb7 2.R×f7 R×f7 3.g6) **2.Q×e6+ Kh8 3.Ne5! K×f4 4.Ng6+! (1–0)**. 4...h×g6 5.h×g6+ R×h4 6.Qe8+ Nf8 7.Q×f8++. **Vysochin-Seletsky**, Ukraine, 2008.

95. **6.Nf5 Qg4** (6...Qh5? 7.Be2 Qg6 8.Nh4) **7.f3 Qg6 8.Nb5**, with a clear advantage for White. The correct move was 5...Nb4.

96. **27.N×d5 Q×a2 28.Nb4! Qa4 29.Nc6!** gains quality, with the double threat to the Rook on d8 and 30.Ra1 winning the Queen (1-0). **Capablanca-Golombek**, Margate, 1939.

97. **38...Ng6! 39.Rh4** (39.Rh6 Nf4+; 39.B×g6 R×e2+ 40.Kf3 R×a2) **39...f5! 40.R×g6 R×g6 41.Bd3 R×e2+ 42.B×e2 a5 43.a4** (43.Bd3 Rg4 44.B×f5 Ra4 45.Bb1 Rb4) **43...Kg7 44.Bb5 Kf6...71** moves **(0–1)**. **G.Kuzmin - Czebe**, European Individual Championship, 11.6.2001.

98. **31.g4! g5 32.h4! Ng6** (32...g×h4 33.g5; 32...g×f4 33.g5) **33.Be4! N×e4 34.h5+ (1–0)**. 34...Kh6 35.R×e4. **Trifunovic-Golombek**, Amsterdam Olympiad, 14.9.1954.

99. **16.Bd6 0-0-0 17.Bb3 h5 18.Qe3 Rhg8 19.Bf4 Qe7** (in view of the threat 20.Bg5) **20.d5! Nc5 21.d6 (1–0)**. **Spassky - Foguelman**, Amsterdam Interzonal, 1964.

100. **12.c4! d×c4** (12...c6 13.Nf4 Nf6 14.Rc1) **13.B×c4+ Kh8 14.Rb1 Qa3 15.Ne5 g6 16.Rb3 Qe7 17.Nf4 Kg7 18.Rh3 Nc6?** (18...Ng5 19.Re3)

19.♘f×g6 (it was even stronger 19.♖×h7+! ♔×h7 20.♘f×g6 ♕d6 21.♘×f8+ ♕×f8 22.♕h5+ ♕h6 23.♗g8+) **19...h×g6 20.♘×g6 ♕f6 21.♘×f8 ♔×f8 22.♖h8+ ♔e7 23.♖h7+ ♔e8 24.♖e1 ♕g6 25.♖f7 ♕×f7 26.♗×f7+ ♔×f7 27.♕h5+ ♔f8 28.♕h6+ ♔f7 29.♕h7+ (1–0).** **Karpov-Pedersen**, Skopje Olympiad, 7.10.1972.

101. In fact, it was reckless. **26.h×g6! h×g6** (26...f×e5 27.♘h5+ ♔g8 28.♕g5 c6 29.g×h7+ ♔h8 30.♕×e5+ and kill in two) **27.♖h5 ♖h8** (27...g×h5 28. ♘×h5+ ♔g8 29.♕h6 ♖f7 30.♗g6 ♖ef8 31.♖e3) **28.♗×g6 ♖eg8 29.♕d3 ♖×h5 30.♘×h5+ ♔f8 31.♘f4 ♘b5 32.g3 ♕c3 33.♕×c3 (1–0). Lyell-Arkell**, Coventry, 17.4.2004.

102. **28.♗×b6+! a×b6 29.♕g1 ♔b8 30.♕×g2 ♘h3 31.♗f1 ♘f4 32.♕d2.** White consolidated, with a two-pawn advantage. **32...♕g5 33.♔b2 h5 34.♖g1 ♕f6 35.♔a1 h4 36.♘e2 ♘g6 37.♕e3 ♖h5 38.♖g2 ♕h8 39.♘c1 ♘e7 40.♖gb2 ♘e8 41.♘d3 ♕h6 (1–0). 42.♕×h6 ♖×h6 43.♘b4. Petrosian-Benko**, Candidates Tournament. Yugoslavia, 11.10.1959.

103. **15.♗c5 ♕h4 16.♖f4 ♕h6 17.♘e4 ♔d8 18.♗e3 g5 19.♖f5 ♕e6 20.♗×g5+ ♔c7 21. 21...♕×f5** (21...♘×c5 22.♗d8+ ♔b8 23.♘×c5 ♕d5 24.♘a6+ b×a6 25.♕b4+) **22.♕d6+ ♔b6 23.♖b1+ ♔a5 24.♕(♗)d2++. Yudovich-Borisenko**, Correspondence, 1964-65.

104. **11.♕c4!** (threatens 12.♘g6/e6+, winning the Queen) **11...g5 12.♕×c7 ♘a6 13.♕d6+ ♔g7 14.♗e3 ♖e8** (14...g×f4 15.♖g1+ ♔h6 16.♗×f4+) **15.0-0-0 (1–0).** 15...g×f4 (15...♖×e3 16.f×e3 g×f4 17.♖hg1+ ♔h6 18.♕f8++) 16.♖hg1+ ♔h8

17.♗d4 ♖e6 18.♕f8++. **Bednarski-Sydor**, Wroclaw, 1972.

105. **14.♘×d5! h×g5 15.♖ac1** (15.♘×e7 ♕d7 16.♘d5 ♘×d5 17.♗×d5 0-0 18.f3) **15...♘×d5 16.♖×c6 b×c6 17.♗×d5 c×d5 18.♕×g7 0-0-0 19.♕e5 (1–0).** **Schebler-Peschel**, Werther, 6.4.2006.

106. **31.♘c5 ♕e7 32.♘×b7 ♕×b7?** (it was forced 32...♔×b7 33.♗×a6) **33.♖c4 ♕×b2 34.♕×b2 ♔×b2 35.♖ad3**, and the trapped piece falls **(1–0). Chekachev-Houhou**, Issy-les-Moulineaux, 27.5.2006.

107. **8.♘d5! ♕d8** (8...c×d5 9.♗×d5 and the Rook on a8 falls) **9.♘×b6! ♕×b6** (9...a×b6 10.♗×f7+) **10.♗×f7+ ♔d7 11.♗×g8**, with a two-pawn advantage and a dominant position. It can follow **11...d5 12.e×d5 ♕×b3** (12...♔×g8 13.d×c6+ ♕×c6 14.♕×g8) **13.d×c6+ ♘×c6 14.♗×b3.**

108. **14...h4 15.♕g4?!** (15.♕×g5 ♕×g5 16.♗×g5 ♘b5 17.♗f6 ♖h6 18.♗g7 c×d3 19.♗×h6 d×e2) **15...♘a4 16.0-0 c×d3 17.c×d3 f5 18.e×f6 ♕×f6 19.♗×g5 ♕f5 20.♕×f5 e×f5 21.♘f4 ♘c6**... 42 moves. **(0–1). Felgaer-Moskalenko**, Barcelona (Cassino), 25.10.2005.

109. **20.♕b7 ♖c7 21.♖fc1!! ♖×b7 22.a×b7 d5** (22...0-0 23.♖c8 ♕×c8 24.b×c8♕ ♖×c8 25.♗×d7 Rogozenko) **23.♖c8 ♗d6 24. 24...♗×f4 25.♖e1+** and mate. **Fridman-Maze**, Marseille, 6.7.2006.

110. **27.b4! ♖a2+** (27...♖a4 28.♔b3 ♗e3 29.♗b2+ ♔f8 30.b5 ♖×c4 31.b×a6 ♖b4+ 32.♔c2 ♖a4 33.♗f6 Atalik) **28.♔b3 ♖×g2 29.b×c5 ♗×c5** (29...♗a1 30.♖d2; 29...♗f6 30.e5 ♗e7 31. c6 ♖b6+ 32.♔c3 ♖b8 33.c7 ♖c8 34.♖b5 Atalik) **30.♖c×c5 ♖b6+?**

(30...♖×h2 31.♖c7 ♖h3+ 32.♔b4 ♖b6+ 33.♔c4 ♖hb3 34.♗d2 Atalik) **31.♖b5 ♖×b5+ 32.♖×b5 ♖×h2 33.♗b2+ (1–0). Atalik-Annageldiev,** Turkey, 2007.

111. **31.♕f2 ♘b3 32.♖e3! (1–0).** 32...♘d4 (32...♘a5 33.b4) 33.♖d3 ♘b3 34.♕f6+! ♔×f6 35.e×f6+ ♔g8 36.♖d8+ ♕f8 37.♖×f8+ ♔×f8 38.c×b3. **Movsesian - Korchnoi,** Carlsbad, 9.9.2007.

112. **23.f4! ♘×d5 (23...♕d6** 24.f×e5 ♗×e5 25.♗×d4 ♗×h2+ 26.♔f1 ♘×d5 27.♗c2) **24.♘×d5 ♔×d5 25.♕×d5 ♘e2+ 26.♔f2 ♕×b2 27.♖a2! ♕×a2 28.♕×a2 ♘c3 29.♕c4 e×f4 30.♗×f4 ♘×d1+ 31.♗×d1 (1–0).** Howell - Mikhalevski, Ottawa, 11.7.2007.

113. **32.g4!** (to activate the Bishop on e1) **32...f×g4** (32...♗×e5 33.d×e5 ♖×e5? 34.♕b2) **33.♗×e4 d×e4 34.♗h4 ♖×e5?!** (34...♖×a7 35.♖×a7 ♕f5 36.♕a2! ♗×e5? 37.d×e5 ♕×e5? 38.♗g3) **35.d×e5 ♗×e5 36.♖f1 ♕g8 37.♗g3! ♗g7** (37...♕×b3?? 38.♖f8+ ♕g8 39.♗×e5++) **38.♕×g8+ (1–0).** 38...♔×g8 39.♗×b8. **Bronstein-Botvinnik,** World Championship (22nd), Moscow, 6.5.1951.

114. **25.♖e4! ♕b5 26.♖a5 ♕b7 27.♘f6+ ♔h8 28.♖h4 ♗c6** (28...♕c7 29.♕d2) **29.♕c1 g5 30.♖×g5 ♘×g5 31.♖×h6+ ♔g7 32.♕×g5+ ♔f8 33.♖h8+ (1–0).** 33...♖e7 34.♕e5++. **Stein-Tarve,** Pärnu, 1971.

115. **11.♗×e4 ♘×c2 12.♗×d5 ♗f5 13.g4 ♗×g4 14.♗e4 ♘×a1 15.♗f4 f5 16.♗d5+ ♔h8 17.♖c1 c6 18.♗g2 ♖fd8 19.♘d2 ♖×d2** (19...h6 20.h4 ♖d3 21.♗f1 ♖d4 22.♗e3 ♖d5 23.♖×a1 ♖×e5 24.♘c4 ♖e4) **20.♗×d2 ♖d8 21.♗c3 ♖d1+ 22.♖×d1 ♗×d1 23.♗f1!.** The Knight has been released,

but the passed pawn and the pair of Bishops give White a clear advantage.

116. **22...♕b6 23.♕g1 d4+ 24.♗g2 ♖fe8 25.h×g4 ♗×g2+ 26.♔×g2 ♕c6+ 27.♔h3 ♖×e1 28.♕×e1 ♖e8 29.♕f1 ♕×c2 30.♗f4 ♖e2 31.♕h1** (31.♕g1? h5 32.♖d1 ♖h2+! 33.♕×h2 h×g4+) **31...h5 32.♖e1?** (32.♕a8+ ♔h7 33.♖h1) **32...♖h2+! 33.♕×h2 h×g4+ 34.♔×g4 ♕×h2** ...49 moves. **(0-1). Klavins-Boleslavsky,** Minsk Zonal, 1957.

117. **26.c5! d×c5** (26...♖f6 27.♘×a7! ♖×a7 28.c×b6 ♖a6 29.♕b5 Golod) **27.♗g8+ ♖×g8 28.♖×d7 ♕g5 29.♗×c5! ♘c6 30.♘c7 ♘b8 31.♘e6 ♕f6** (31...♕g6 32.♘f8+ ♖×f8 33.♗×f8 ♘×d7 34.♖×d7 f4 35.h3; 31...♕h5 32.♖d8 ♕g6 33.♖×b8 ♕×e6 34. ♗e3 Golod) **32.♘×g7 ♘×g7 33.♗e7 ♕g6 34.♖×a7 b5 35.♕c2 ♔h8?** (35...♘c6 36.♖a6 ♖c8 37.♗a3) **36.♖d6 ♘e6 37.g3 ♘d4 38.♖×g6 (1–0). Golod-Huschenbeth,** Hamburg, 11.3.2008.

118. **25.d5! e×d5 26.♘d4 ♗×f6 27.e×f6 ♕d6 28.♗×c6 ♕×f6 29.♗×d7 ♕×d4 30.g3 ♕c5 31.♕×c5 b×c5 32.♗c6 d4 33.♗b5 ♔f8 34.f4 g×f4 35.g×f4 (1–0). Carlsen-Ivanchuk,** Morelia/Linares, 6.3.2007.

119. **24.♗h6+!! ♔×h6** (24...♔h8 25.♗×f8 ♘cd7 26.♗×d6) **25.♕e3+ ♔g7 26.♕e7+ ♔h6 27.♕×f8+ ♔h5 28.♕×f6,** with a decisive advantage. Variant analysis of the game **Zakhartsov-Gochelashvili,** Maikop 2008.

120. **27.♘×h6! ♕g5 28.♕f3! ♕×h6 29.♗d2!** (29.♖×f8+ ♖×f8 30.♕×f8 ♔h7 31.♕×d6 ♗e4) **29...♕×f4 30.♗×f4 ♖e8 31.a×b5 a×b5 32.♕c6 ♔h7** (not 32...b4 33.♗×d6 ♖e6 34.♕c8) **33.♕×b5 d5 34.♕d7 d4**

35.h4! Re4 36.Bg3 Be7 37.h5 Bxh5 (37...Re1+ 38.Kh2 Bxh5 39.f3 Re2 40.b4 c4 41.b5 d3 42.b6) **38.f3 Re2 39.Kf1 Rxb2 40.Qxe7 Rb1+ 41.Kf2 (1–0). Karjakin-Bacrot**, Wijk aan Zee, 19.1.2006.

121. **14...Bd6! 15.Qxh8 Qxg5 16.f4** (16.Qxh7 Bf5 17.Rd5 Ke6) **16...Qh4 17.Rxe4 Bh3! 18.Qxa8 Bc5+ 19.Kh1 Bxg2+ 20.Kxg2 Qg4+ (0–1).** 21.Kf1 Qf3+ 22.Ke1 Qf2++. **Euwe-Réti**, Amsterdam, 1920.

122. **1.e7! Re4+ 2.Kf1** (2.Kd1 Rxe5 3.Nd6 Rxe7 4.Nf5 Re5) **2...Rxe5 3.Nc7 Rxe7 4.Nd5! Re5** (4...Re8/e4 5.Nf6+; 4...Rd7 5.Nf6+) **5.Nf4+ Kg4 6.Nd3**, followed by **7.Nxe1** and a draw. Study by **M. Perelman** (1955).

123. **30.Ne4 Qe7 31.Nf6+ Kf7 32.Nxh7 Kg8 33.Nf6+ Kf7 34.Ng4! Kg8 35.Qd2 Re8 36.Qf4 Qd6 37.Qf2! Qc5 38.Qg3 Qd4** (38...Qe7 39.Qf3 Rc8 40.Qf4 Qd6 41.Qd4 Qe7 42.Nf6+ Kf7 43.Ne4 Kg8 44.d6 Krasenkow) **39.Kh2! Nd8 40.Qd6! Ne6 41.Be3! (1–0).** The black Queen can't stay on the d–file and continue defending f6. **Topalov-Shirov**, Wijk aan Zee, 16.1.2007.

124. **32...Qc8!** (threat 33...Qa8) **33.Nac1** (33.Nc5 Rxc5 34.dxc5 Qa8 35.Qb3 Ra3 36.Qc2 Ne5, followed by ...Nd3) **33...Bxb4 34.Qd3 Bd6 35.Rb1 h5 36.Nb3 h4** ...55 moves. **(0–1). Benko-Petrosian**, Los Angeles, 18.7.1963.

125. **23.Re1! Bxf3 24.gxf3 Nf5 25.Re5 Nd4 26.Nc4! Ne6** (26...Nxf3 27.Rxc5 Nxh2 28.a4) **27.a4 Ra8 28.b3 Ra5 29.Kb2 Kf8 30.Nxe6 fxe6 31.Rxe6 c4 32.Re4 cxb3 33.Bxb3 Rh5 34. h4 Rf5 35.f4 Rh5 36.Kb4 Rxh4 37.a5 Rh1 38.a6 Kf7 39.Ka5**

Rd1 40.a7 Rd8 41.Rb4 Ra8 42.Ka6 Ke6 43.Rb5 Rf8 44.f5+ Kd7 45.Rb7+ (1–0). Grischuk-Volokitin, Russian Team Championship, 5.5.2007.

126. **17.0-0-0! Qxf3 18.Qxe7! Qe2** (18...Rb4 19.Nf6+ Qxf6 20.Qxf6 gxf6 21.Bf5 Ra8 22.Rhg1+ Kh8 23.Kd2 Rb2+ 24.Kc2) **19.Nf6+ (1–0).** 19...gxf6 20.Rhg1+ Kh8 21.Qxf8++. **Magomedov-Willemze**, Moscow, 2008.

127. **47.Kh2! Rh5** (47...Kd8 48.Ra8+ Bc8 49.Ba6+; 47...Ke6 48.f5+Ke7 49.b5+-) **48.b5!** (48.Be2? Rh4 49.b5 Rxf4=) **48...Rxc5 49.Bxh3 f5 50.bxc6 Rxc6 51.Bxf5 Rd6 52.Kg3! Ke8 53.Rxd7 Rxd7 54.Bxd7+ Kxd7 55.Kg4 Ke6 56.Kg5 Kf7 57.Kf5 (1–0). Tal-Trifunovic**, Palma de Mallorca 1968. It was the only time Tal beat GM Trifunovic.

128. **17.Qg4!! Qxa1** (17...Nxb3 18.Qxe6+ Be7 19.Bg5 +-) **18.Bxe6 Rd8 19.Bh6! Qc3** (unique, according to Kasparov; if 19...Qxf1+ 20.Kxf1 gxh6, 21.Qh5+ and mate) **20.Bxg7 Qd3 21.Bxh8 Qg6** (21...Ne2+ 22.Kh1 Ng3+ 23.hxg3 Qxf1+ 24.Kh2 Qd3 25.Bf5! Qc4 [25...Qd1 26.f3 +-] 26.f4 Qxa2 27.Bxh7 +- Ftacnik) **22.Bf6 Be7 23.Bxe7 Qxg4** (23...Kxe7 24.Qh4+ Ke8 25.Bg4 +-) **24.Bxg4 Kxe7 25.Rc1! c6 26.f4 a5 27.Kf2 a4 28.Ke3 b4 29.Bd1 a3 30.g4 (+-) 30...Rd5 31.Rc4 c5** (31...Nf5+ 32.gxf5 Rxd1 33.f6+ Kd7 34.Rxb4) **32.Ke4 Rd8 33.Rxc5 Ne6 34.Rd5 Rc8 35.f5 Rc4+ 36.Ke3 Nc5 37.g5 Rc1 38.Rd6 (1–0). Kasparov-Anand**, PCA World Championship (10th), New York 26.9.1995.

www.ingramcontent.com/pod-product-compliance
Lightning Source LLC
La Vergne TN
LVHW060358200726
843506LV00003B/259

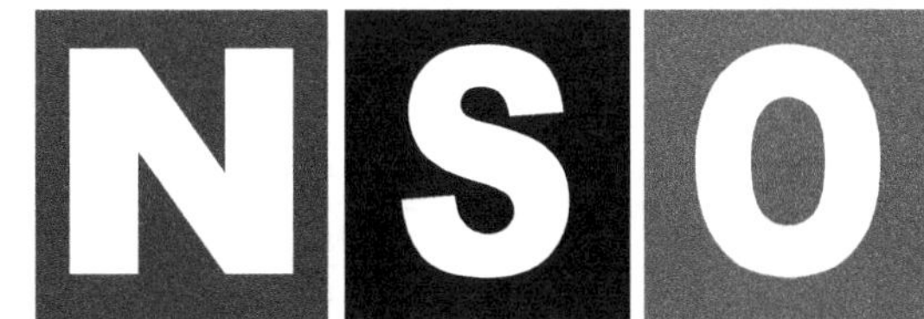

OLYMPIAD WORKBOOK

NATIONAL SCIENCE OLYMPIAD

01 Learning Objectives

02 Multiple Choice Questions

03 HOTS (Achievers Section)

04 Model Test Paper

05 Answer Keys and Solutions

06 OMR Answer Sheet

V&S PUBLISHERS

Published by:

V&S PUBLISHERS

F-2/16, Ansari road, Daryaganj, New Delhi-110002
☎ 23240026, 23240027 • *Fax:* 011-23240028
✉ info@vspublishers.com • 🌐 www.vspublishers.com

Online Brandstore: amazon.in/vspublishers

Regional Office : Hyderabad
5-1-707/1, Brij Bhawan (Beside Central Bank of India Lane)
Bank Street, Koti, Hyderabad - 500 095
☎ 040-24737290
✉ vspublishershyd@gmail.com

Follow us on:   

BUY OUR BOOKS FROM: AMAZON FLIPKART

© **Copyright:** V&S PUBLISHERS
ISBN 978-81-977761-9-9
New Edition